THE
CROOKED
PATH

SHIRLEY J. GILBERT, Ph.D.

Printed in the United States of America

ISBN: Softcover   978-1-63871-382-1
        eBook   978-1-63871-383-8

Republished by: PageTurner Press and Media LLC
Publication Date: 07/28/2021

To order copies of this book, contact:

PageTurner Press and Media
Phone: 1-888-447-9651
info@pageturner.us
www.pageturner.us

TABLE OF CONTENTS

INTRODUCTION

Life brings most of us to thoughtful crooked paths of wonder. It leads the thoughtful person on a path of many windings. We live our lives forward but often understand them better when we view them in retrospect. This is true of Sam's story.

The twists and turns of our journey often feel out of our control. Yet, we are always left with making a choice about how we are going to respond or react to them. In essence, this is what determines the shape of the crooked path.

There probably isn't anyone who manages to have a life with a straight path. The journey is much more complex for most people. We never know what the impact of our journey will be as others cross our path. Parts of the crooked path are our most treasured pieces and others are parts we wish had never happened. All of these pieces come together to form each person's unique crooked path.

As people travel their journey, different things become more important than others depending on when and where they are on the path. Childhood issues are much different than end of life issues. All of it goes into forming the crooked path. We must own it all.

Probably the most important piece of the journey over which we have control is our ability to respond to the events on our crooked path. We can't change the event, but we can choose how to respond. This fact can change lives.

It changed Sam's.

CHAPTER 1

I'm Just A Little Boy

The last thing Sam remembered was falling asleep in the back seat as he and his family were driving home from a Christmas program at his school.

It was a 30 minute drive back to their farm and the snow was falling steadily. It had been a beautiful crisp December day. The family had enjoyed a favorite meal together that day. Sam's mom loved to cook and the family loved to eat. It had been a nearly perfect day.

By the time the program was over at the school, the weather had taken a big turn for the worse. There were nearly blizzard conditions on the roads. Getting home would not be easy. Finally, they were only five miles from home. They were very close to their turn off. On the last major hill before exiting the highway, everything changed.

Sam's dad was an excellent driver, but could do nothing as he watched the big rig sliding sideways down the middle of the road on black ice coming right toward them. He swerved sharply but could not avoid the collision. Sam's mother and two sisters were ejected from the car as it slammed into the huge semi. The sound of crunching metal could be heard in all directions.

When Sam woke up, the car was upside down in a steep gully. His father was bleeding and unconscious. Sam was only five years old and had no idea how to help his dad. He started to cry. It was more than two hours before anyone found them. Sam was freezing and hysterical. He was taken by ambulance to the nearest hospital. He had a broken arm and a concussion. His mother and sisters had not survived. His father was in intensive care, in a coma.

After two weeks in the hospital, Sam was discharged to his mother's sister and her family, Aunt Sadie and Uncle George. They had two daughters and lived on a farm near Sam's. Before leaving, Sam was taken to his father's hospital room. He was now conscious but still in intensive care. It would be a lengthy recovery. Both he and Sam were reeling emotionally from the deaths of their beloved family members. Funerals had been held without them. Their lives would never be the same. Sam wept convulsively as he hugged his dad and left the hospital.

It was on that January day that Sam's life took a huge fork in the road. He was now in unknown territory, far outside of his comfort zone. His grief was enormous and he felt desperately hopeless.

Aunt Sadie, Uncle George, Sara and Sidney were all very welcoming to Sam. Aunt Sadie and his mother were twins. They were and had always been very close sisters.

They had prepared a special room for him with new curtains, linens, bedspread and stuffed animals. They had shopped for him and bought him some new clothes. In time, they would take him back to the farm where he could collect some of his things. For now, he would need to try to adjust to his new life.

Sara and Sidney were eight and ten years old. They really liked the idea of having a little brother (even though they knew he was their cousin). They were all very nice to him and treated him like the family member that he was.

Sam loved animals and was especially drawn to the bunnies and the sheep on the farm. He loved to ride the pony, Zipper. He and his cousins spent many hours outside, making chores fun and always taking time to enjoy the animals. They took turns riding their pony. Sam was adjusting.

The hardest part of the day for Sam was bedtime. That was when he thought most about his mom. She had always tucked him in at night. It had been their special time. Aunt Sadie understood this and made it a point to read Sam a story every night. She even took him shopping and let him pick out his favorite books. She and her family were making every effort to support Sam and help him heal from his trauma. He was lucky to have them.

Sam started back to school. This was a huge adjustment for him. The kids treated him differently now. He didn't like it. It seemed everyone felt sorry for him. He had one friend, Luke, who didn't treat him that way. They were best buddies. Sam relied on Luke every day to make school a pleasant place for him. Sam was very bright, made good grades and was liked by his teachers. Very slowly, he was establishing a new normal for himself. He hated that his life would never be the way it once was. There was really no one who could turn back the clock, not even God.

After school that day when he got home, his Aunt Sadie asked him if he wanted to go back to his farm and get some of his personal things. He took a deep breath and said he did. They got in the car and headed to his home. Sam began to cry. It was as though a tsunami of grief hit his little heart and overwhelmed him. He just couldn't manage it right now.

Aunt Sadie turned the car around and they returned home. Sam wasn't ready. She wasn't certain when he would ever be ready but it wasn't now. She was sad to see how overwhelmed he had become at just the thought of returning to his home. She looked forward to discussing this when she and Sam saw his psychologist that week. Social services had arranged for Sam to have as many therapy sessions as he needed to process his losses and establish some solid new beginnings. Some weeks it looked like an impossible dream.

Sam's dad was finally out of intensive care but remained in the hospital. He suffered a major concussion, several broken ribs and a broken hip. He also had crushed two vertebrae in his back and two in his neck. He was in severe pain. Sam saw him once a week for a very short period of time, but it helped him just to see and know that his dad was still alive and making progress, albeit slowly.

Seeing Sam was also a comfort to his dad. His physical needs were so great he had little energy to give to his grief and emotional issues. He was fighting for his life.

As they left the hospital that day, Sam asked if they could stop by his house on the way home. Aunt Sadie locked eye contact with him and asked him if he was really up to it. He said he was.

As they pulled into the farm, Sam took a hard look at it. It felt strange to him. It felt different. He climbed the stairs, went in and went directly to his room. It was exactly the same as he had left it. Quietly and methodically, he grabbed a sack and put a few things in it. What seemed most important to him was his teddy bear. He had once told his mom that sometimes in the middle of the night when he woke up and was scared, he would hug his bear and pretend it was her. The bear was a comfort to him and he was happy to get it back. He also took a favorite book his mother used to read to him. He loved the story of Hansel and Gretel. All of this took him less than ten minutes and he told Aunt Sadie he was ready to leave.

Even more than what Sam had gathered to take with him was the strength he showed in being able to be there. This was great progress for him.

When they arrived home, Sam took his things to his room, unpacked them and smiled as he put his teddy bear on his bed. This seemed to mean the most to him. Somehow it made his mother's presence very real to him. He loved and felt comforted by that feeling.

It was Spring now. The animals were having babies. He loved watching the baby lambs grow up. He and Zipper, the pony, had become buddies and he rode him almost every day when he came home from school. He was settling into a kind of a routine and his life seemed to be coming together.

Sam was turning six on Sunday. The family was planning to make it a special celebration for him. Part of that specialness included a trip to his father's bedside that day. They wouldn't stay long. They just wanted to include him. They thought it would mean a lot to Sam.

Aunt Sadie baked his favorite cake and planned the menu around his favorite foods. His birthday gift was a new bicycle. He had never had one of his own. He loved it! There was plenty of room for him to ride it at the farm.

Sam was slowly making a healthy adjustment to a life he was enjoying. He was doing well in school, kept his weekly appointments with the school psychologist, had regular visits to see his dad and enjoyed his new family. He was used to having two big sisters. He was making a healthy adjustment

His next big challenge would include a trip to the cemetery to visit the gravesites of his mother and his sisters. This would likely not occur anytime soon. In fact, it would probably be best if he made this trip with his dad.

His dad was finally discharged from the hospital. He went to physical therapy three times each week. He was slowly getting better. He had moved back to the farm. He was having a very difficult time adjusting. In fact, he started having panic attacks. He had intense and violent episodes. They felt like the end of the world to him. He felt terrified as he fought all of the horrific flashbacks from the accident. In fact, he just wanted to be out of there and never look back. He was beginning to wish he had also died in the accident. He was severely depressed.

Sam was not visiting his dad anymore. Sometimes they would talk by telephone. Sam really didn't want to return to the farm. It was just too hard for him. Also, his dad just didn't seem the same to him anymore. It was as though his entire family was dead. He wondered why he survived.

Early on a Sunday morning, the phone rang. Uncle George answered. It was 5AM. It was the county sheriff. He disclosed that Sam's father's body had been discovered. He had ended his life in the kitchen with a bullet through his head. He was dead.

Sam was now ten years old, much too young to understand his father's actions. This child had already been through much too much trauma. How would he ever survive this?

Sadie and George spent the entire day trying to decide how they were going to handle this event. How were they going to tell a ten year old trauma survivor that his father had just blown his head off because he didn't want to live anymore?

They finally decided they needed to protect Sam. They would make up a story. They would not even share the truth with their own children. Sam's dad had to go to a rehabilitation facility on the east coast. He would live there permanently. He had to be transferred before Sam could tell him goodbye. It was simply the way it was. The farm would be sold and it would be put in a trust for Sam when he reached 18 years old.

The last time Sam had seen his dad was the day they visited the cemetery. They didn't stay long. They laid some flowers on each of the three graves. Their pastor had gone with them and said a brief prayer. It felt pretty surreal to Sam. He did not feel much of anything nor did he show any emotion. He felt numb. They were almost a distant memory now.

*****

Sam's young life has been nothing short of traumatic. As if childhood had not been hard enough, he has lost most of his family and was nearly killed in a violent and traumatic accident which he would never forget. What a difficult beginning.

Fortunately, Sam had a back-up family. Not everyone does. He was young enough that he adjusted to being part of another family. Nonetheless, there would always be a part of him that would embrace the life he once knew. There was no going back.

The trauma of that violent accident has predisposed Sam to being a sensitive child. He lived with trauma that most of us have never known. He had learned already that life was very unpredictable and that it makes requirements of all of us that are beyond difficult.

He needed to find his own way, his own crooked path.

CHAPTER 2

New Beginnings

Now that Sam had settled into his aunt and uncle's family, they asked if he would like to change his last name to theirs. He liked the idea very much. They formally adopted him. By now, he was very comfortable in his new family and grateful to be part of it. He enjoyed his life and was happy to have bonded with such loving people. He would miss his dad but was prepared to accept the reality of his need to move far away. He was only ten years old and had a lot on his little mind.

Through the next several years, there were many happy events in his new family. As time passed, he had a hard time really remembering what his life had been for the first five years. This was his new family and his new reality. He loved it.

The years went by quickly. Finally Sam was a senior in high school. One more month and he would be graduating. He was turning eighteen very soon. Little did he know that his trust fund would be coming available to him. He would be able to attend college if he wanted. In fact, he could do just about whatever he wanted.

Sadie and George made a momentous decision that it was time to tell Sam the truth about his father's death.

They realized that it might have serious consequences about how he would feel about the fact they had lied to him. It could be devastating for them. Nonetheless, they felt they owed him the truth.

It was a Saturday morning. Sadie had prepared Sam's favorite breakfast. After they were finished eating, George told him they had something they needed to tell him.

The next four hours were gruelling for each of them. Sam was shocked and horrified. He was upset on several levels. He was deeply troubled that no one had come to his father's aid and helped him get through those dark days. He was upset with Sadie and George for not telling him the truth, although he could appreciate their reasons. He was upset that no one trusted him enough to be honest with him and help him manage the truth.

They also told him about the money. He had acquired a very large sum of money that belonged exclusively to him. They would take him to the bank, open an account and deposit it.

At the close of the conversation, both Sadie and George offered their tearful apologies, emphasizing they knew what they did was wrong but, in their minds, it was to protect him. Sam merely nodded and left the table.

This was the second time in Sam's life that he felt totally traumatized. It was as though he had lost two families in eighteen years. He felt as though he was starting a brand new chapter of his life.

Graduation was in two weeks. That would give him time to solidify his financial funds and make some plans to leave the farm and go…..somewhere.

Sam felt beyond betrayed. It seemed his whole life was nothing but trauma, sadness and lies. What a way to feel. Graduation was supposed to represent some kind of achievement. For Sam, he felt he was celebrating survival and he was not happy about it.

Graduation came and went. He didn't even return to the farm that night. He spent the night on a bench at the train station. He just wanted to get on the next train and keep going. He had no idea why and he didn't care where. He just wanted to put as much distance as he could between himself and that town. He wanted to let it go and never look back. He felt "done."

Sam gave the clerk at the window of the train station two crisp $100 bills and asked how far away that would get him. Sam really didn't care. He just needed to know he was headed away from that town. He knew he had to clear his head and had no idea how long or how many miles that would require. He had never felt more alone.

He boarded the train, took a seat in the last row and rested his head against the window. Soon, he was sound asleep. When he awakened, he was staring at an unbelievably beautiful coast line. He made his way to the dining car and ordered a big breakfast. The food was surprisingly excellent. The scenery was beautiful. After a few minutes, a girl was seated across from him. She was very attractive. She smiled at him and said, "Good morning, I'm Natalie." He returned the smile and nodded, "Sam."

She ordered breakfast and told Sam she was on her way to a seminar. She was a law student and was getting ready to take the Bar Exam. Although she had been a good student, she was feeling very nervous about whether or not she could pass. It was her goal to become an attorney and specialize in helping children. She appeared to be a compassionate person.

Sam was happy to have some company that morning. He didn't mind at all listening to Natalie talk about her law school experiences and her future goals. Actually, it was refreshing. It took his mind off of himself. Natalie was getting off at the next stop. Sam appreciated that she didn't ask him any personal questions. He was not ready to answer anyone's questions.

Following breakfast, Sam moved to the section of the train with the large windows, the dome car. It was excellent for viewing the landscape. He spent the entire day there, just taking in the beauty of the earth, wondering about the lives of people who lived in the houses he saw. He was actually contemplating if there was anyone else in the world who felt as lost as he did.

As the evening wore on, Sam made himself comfortable in the dome car, covered himself with a blanket and forced his mind to think of pleasant thoughts, relax and enjoy the ride. He had a restless night. He was painfully aware that he was on a train and had no idea where it was going . He really didn't even care. This scared him. Somehow, he needed to find some form of stability in his life. Right now, he was running away and it felt like the only choice he had.

That morning, the train arrived in Seattle. The conductor pointed out to Sam that it was as far as his ticket would take him. He was forced to get off the train. Sam had never been to Seattle. He knew it rained a lot there. He loved the rain. He found a cafe near the train station and decided to have breakfast.

While he was eating, he got a newspaper and started reading the classified section. He really didn't have any skills but he did have a high school education. He was young and strong and surely he could be of use to someone somewhere. He wanted a job more than he needed one. He had plenty of money. What he needed was a purpose.

Sam figured Seattle was as good a place as any to try to start a new life. He needed a job and a place to live. He would let the days unfold and take it just one day at a time. He was hanging onto hope.

*****

Sam made the decision to get on a train and trust where it was taking him. The dye had been cast. He was determined to figure out his life on his own.

He had financial resources since the farm had been sold. He could actually survive for quite a while without getting a job. Nonetheless, he wanted to find a place where he could feel good about himself and his choices. Right now he was just feeling very vulnerable and needy.

He just wanted a chance to lick his wounds and decide for himself how he could navigate his crooked path.

Sam actually demonstrated confidence in his ability to strike out on his own and forge a life for himself. He had been a survivor for a long time. What he was trying to do now wasn't nearly as difficult as what he had already endured. Somehow he had the confidence to believe that he would find a way to make a life for himself.

Even though Sam had left the farm with very resentful feelings toward his aunt and uncle, deep down he realized all they had done for him. He didn't hate them, he just needed some space right now to clear his head and find his way. Somewhere down the road he believed he would be able to resolve the conflict. Now wasn't that time.

Although Sam had constructed a very difficult challenge for himself, he was not without tools to make it happen. He had survived trauma and lost his family but had years of a happy life with people who loved him.

Sam had done well in school. He was well-liked and had a lot of friends. He had been highly socialized and knew how to get along with people. He had known love and support. It just felt like it was time to put it all to good use, in his way, in his timing. He was, in fact, continuing to create his crooked path.

CHAPTER 3

A Roof and Some Food

As Sam was reading the classified section, he saw an immediate ad for a paper boy. They needed someone to start delivering papers that week. It was nothing like what he wanted but it might be a way to survive until he could find a real job. After all, he had money from selling the farm. He didn't need to panic.

Sam rented a cheap room and began delivering papers. He checked the newspaper every day and was beginning to get discouraged. One day he came across an ad that read, "part time position for junior assistant." There were no details about the position. Sam had no idea if he knew how to be an assistant but knew he needed to learn a trade of some kind.. Maybe he could take this job and continue his paper route. He would at least inquire. There was only a phone number.

Sam dialed the number on his cell phone. A man answered. He sounded like an older man. He was the one looking for an assistant. He asked Sam to tell him a bit about himself. Sam coiled inside. He wasn't eager to share any part of his life with anyone. He simply shared that he was a recent high school graduate who had just arrived in the city and was looking for a job. The man followed up with a few questions. Finally, he and Sam set up an appointment for a meeting later that afternoon.

As he hung up, Sam was thinking he couldn't believe what he had just done. He must be as desperate as he thought he was.

Sam hadn't had a haircut in a month. He knew he needed to shower, shave and put on some decent clothes. He made himself presentable. He was on his way to meet the man who needed a junior assistant part time.

Sam was certain he must have misunderstood the address. He was standing outside of a beautiful wrought iron gate with a very long driveway which led to what looked like a large mansion. Hesitantly, he pushed the button on the panel and announced he was there to see "Arthur." To his surprise, the man identified himself as Arthur and the large gate opened.

He rang the bell and heard the chimes ring in the house. Slowly, the door opened and he found himself standing in front of an elderly man in a wheelchair. He identified himself as Arthur, extended his hand warmly and invited Sam into his home.

Once inside, Arthur directed Sam to join him in his study. It was a gorgeous room, cherry wood panelling throughout, a whole wall of books, a large leather chair, polished pewter, a large chandelier and a beautiful oak desk. This man was obviously good at something. Sam was becoming more interested by the minute.

Arthur introduced himself. He was a retired litigation attorney. He had retired a decade ago and had written several books. His home had 12 bedrooms, 9 bathrooms, 6 fireplaces, a theater, a sauna, a swimming pool, a stable, an elevator and 2 kitchens on 26 acres. He had a butler, a chauffeur, a cook, a gardener, a nurse and a doctor on retainer. He did not appear to be a man with any needs.

Arthur had rubbed elbows with the best litigators in the world, had been recognized as one of the best legal minds of the 21st century and had enjoyed a rich life. Now he found himself facing end of life issues and looking for a way to effectively manage this phase of his life. He was now a legal consultant for a few good friends who were still high-powered litigators.

Arthur had never married, and had no children or grandchildren. Also, he was an only child so he had no nieces or nephews. He had no one except for his employees, a few friends and hundreds of acquaintances.

He realized Sam was young for this position and had no legal expertise. However, he was just looking for someone to perform some very basic tasks. He might be teachable and capable. He would give him a try for thirty days. That should be long enough to see if he could cut it. Time would tell.

Although he didn't share this fact with Sam, Arthur was open to the idea of mentoring a worthy person wanting to learn. He was no longer trafficking in the big leagues. He just needed an assistant to help him proofread and assist in assembling his legal briefs. He explained this to Sam. He described the work as predictably boring. He asked how he felt about learning about legal matters. Sam admitted he didn't know much about it but was open to learning.

As the conversation progressed, Sam began to better understand what it was Arthur needed. Sam had made decent grades in school and this job description sounded like something he could do. The pay wasn't great, but he could use it while he looked for something else. For sure, he didn't want to be a farmer!

With hesitancy on both sides, they agreed to a month-long trial. Sam would be expected to work four hours per day, five days per week for thirty days. The days would include Tuesday, Wednesday, Thursday, Friday and Sunday. They shook hands and Sam assured him he would see him the next morning promptly at 8 A.M.

When Sam questioned the days he was to work, Arthur made it clear that his duties would be solely dependent on Arthur's needs on that particular day. Arthur did stipulate that he wanted Sam to drive him each Sunday to his church. Although church had never been a part of Sam's life, he agreed. It would simply be part of the job description. Besides, he would get paid for it.

Sam could hardly believe what had just happened to him. He had left a town where he had lived his whole life, gotten on a train without knowing the destination, was now in Seattle and had just found what he hoped would be a better job than delivering newspapers. It was all very surreal.

Sam treated himself to a nice dinner that night. He went to bed feeling focused and ready for a new challenge. He felt extremely grateful for the events of the day.

At 8 a.m. Arthur greeted him at the front door and they went directly to the study. The cook brought in fresh coffee and a light breakfast. Arthur said he needed assistance putting together a legal brief, a project where he had agreed to be a legal consultant. Sam looked at Arthur and smiled. "Just tell me what to do."

Throughout the morning, Arthur directed Sam in helping him assemble the pieces of constructing a brief. The entire experience was a teaching moment for Sam. He was genuinely enjoying the expertise of Arthur. The man was beyond brilliant. This was an amazing educational experience for Sam. In fact, it crossed his mind to wonder what it might actually be like to be an attorney.

They broke for lunch. They had a sandwich and sat outside by the pool. It was a sunny day. Their conversation was superficial. Sam questioned Arthur about the house, and his career. Sam made certain to keep the focus on Arthur. He wasn't ready to share anything personal about himself.

Arthur expressed to Sam that someday he hoped these grounds would house some kind of worthy foundation that would help others. He wasn't at all sure what that would be. He had thought long and hard about it and wanted it to be some kind of haven for helping people, but he wasn't sure who he wanted to help.

Sunday morning, Sam drove Arthurs's car as they headed off to church. This was unknown territory for Sam. He had never understood the mind of God. He wasn't interested in a God who would have allowed such traumatic events in Sam's early life. He was there strictly for Arthur. He kept these feelings to himself.

The month went by very quickly. Sam felt he had learned a great deal about legal issues. He felt very grateful for his new knowledge and was genuinely enjoying it. He had balanced his two jobs comfortably. He was managing his time well. So far, so good. He appreciated Arthur's treatment of him and found him to be an excellent teacher. He was very patient with him.

When the month ended, Arthur asked Sam whether or not he was interested in extending his employment. Without hesitation, Sam emphatically agreed! They agreed to extend it for 6 months, still on a part-time basis, still at a very low salary.

The next 6 months flew by. Sam was getting the hang of what Arthur needed to prepare his briefs. He was gaining a lot of respect for Arthur's knowledge and the way he used it to help others. He had a rich history of taking on some very tough legal challenges and winning all of them. He was a legend. Sam had looked him up on the internet.

At the end of the 6 months, Arthur inquired of Sam if he had any interest in learning more about legal matters. Sam said he would need to think about it. They agreed to have a conversation about it at the end of the week.

On the last day of their employment agreement, Arthur brought up their continuing conversation about a possible legal career. As Sam pondered this throughout the week, he realized the only 'profession' he had observed in his family was that of farming. He was certain he wanted no part of that.

He never had dreams of becoming anything as a young boy. He was simply focused on surviving. Now, maybe fate was giving him a chance. This was a window of unexpected opportunity he knew would not always be available to him. Since it was the only real opportunity he had right now, he decided to go for it!

Arthur and Sam forged an agreement that he could live in the house and continue to assist Arthur from now until he was a bona fide attorney. He would have a very small stipend and would need to continue his time commitment to Arthur and his projects. Sam agreed. So now, he would quit his paper route, continue working for Arthur and go to school. After he graduated law school, he would be required to give Arthur one full year of his time without any salary. After that he could decide how he swanted to plan his life. Arthur drew up a contract which they both signed

Sam worked harder than he ever had. He flew through two years of college through courses on the internet. He had plans for completing the last two in one year. Then, he could actually start law school right there in Seattle. He had fallen into an ideal setting with an ideal mentor. Was something good finally happening to him? This felt almost too good to be true.

*****

Sam and Arthur were at the beginning of working out a relationship that would benefit them both. This was a greater opportunity than Sam ever could have envisioned. He sometimes asked himself if he could really be this lucky. Arthur had offered him the chance of a lifetime. He was doing his very best, both for himself and for Arthur.

Arthur saw something in Sam that Sam didn't see in himself. He believed Sam had the makings of becoming a competent and successful attorney. Sam was beyond grateful that he had found someone like Arthur to be his mentor, someone who believed in him.

Sam didn't allow himself to look back on his life. He was determined to focus forward and reach his goal. He felt he would be without excuse if he didn't reach it. Had he really been this lucky or was someone looking out for him? He had no idea. Regardless, he was determined to succeed.

Sam was aware that a good part of his drive to succeed was his desire to please Arthur. He seemed like the grandfather Sam had never had. Sam was starting to feel bonded with Arthur in a way that surprised him. Apart from his mother, he had never really felt bonded to anyone.

This was a teaching moment in his life, in more ways than one. Little did he realize the crooked path he was navigating. It would be a challenge to find and keep the balance.

CHAPTER 4

Law School

A rthur's library proved to be invaluable to Sam. He spent long hours there on his own time reading and applying what he read. Arthur was a phenomenal coach and helped him ace every quiz and exam. They were developing a kind of easy and respectful relationship. Sam had never had a grandfather but he envisioned it might have been something like this.

As time went on, Sam was becoming a more valuable aid to Arthur and was taking on more responsibility. Arthur could communicate now in legal terms which Sam understood. He was eager to learn. It seemed to come naturally to him. Arthur had no doubts about Sam becoming an exemplary attorney. He was sharp as a tack. The beauty of it for Arthur was that he always had an assistant for whatever he was working on. It was a bit of a symbiotic relationship. Right now, it worked for both of them.

Finally, Sam was in his last year of law school and beginning to study for the Bar Exam. He was excited. He had enjoyed this experience so much. He felt so privileged to have his very own private tutor. Arthur's coaching had been as valuable as anything he had learned in the classroom. He had never had a mentor, certainly never dreamed of having one of this caliber. For the first time in his life, he actually felt 'blessed.'

One evening, after an especially productive day, Arthur and Sam had a delightful dinner and Sam's favorite dessert. In an unexpected moment, after a few glasses of wine, Arthur expressed to Sam how gratifying it had been for him to have mentored him and how proud he was of him. Sam took a deep gulp and his eyes teared up. He hated it when he got emotional.

Totally, without provocation, Sam shared the basics of his life story with Arthur. He described the violent accident and trauma when he was 5 years old. He explained what happened to his family and that he was raised by his mother's sister and family. He added the part of being lied to and the response he had. He explained getting on the train, ending up in Seattle, seeing his ad and coming to work with him.

Arthur didn't say anything. He simply looked at Sam in amazement. He said, "I always knew there was some kind of deep pain in your life but I knew you would tell me if you wanted me to know......thank you for trusting me." When Sam stood to leave the table, he bent over and gave Arthur a very warm hug and said, "No..... thank YOU!"

As Sam went back to his room, he had deep feelings of gratitude and respect for Arthur. He had earned Sam's trust, something Sam wasn't sure any man could ever do again.

That Sunday when they went to church, for the first time Sam thanked God for bringing Arthur into his life. Clearly, he was a God-send. Maybe his mother sent him. Somehow, he felt watched over, cared for, nurtured, protected and loved. He could never remember having any of these feelings before now. Maybe this was the God who directed crooked paths. Maybe this was the beginning of Sam's healing.

For the first time in years, Sam thought of Aunt Sadie and Uncle George. Somehow, he felt the urge to contact them. They hadn't heard from him in many years. He still remembered their phone number from long ago. He had no idea if they would even want to talk with him after all of this time.

Aunt Sadie answered the phone. Sam took a deep breath and simply said, "Hi, it's Sam." There was a very pregnant pause at the other end. Finally, with a broken voice and a broken heart she said, "Sam, I can't believe it's you."

Sam apologized for leaving like he did and for never contacting them through the years after all they did for him. He asked about each member of the family and waited for her response. "I lost George two years ago. He had a sudden heart attack and passed quickly. We so regretted the way we handled the death of your father. We realized quickly that we managed it all wrong. We were heartbroken. The girls are doing well. They are both married and each have one child. They miss you. We all miss you."

Sam responded by saying he would like to come and visit them but he wanted to wait until he finished his schooling. He told her he was graduating law school. She was shocked and thrilled. He said he would explain things when he saw her. They both agreed how good it felt to finally connect. Sam gave her his phone number. They agreed to keep in touch until he made his visit. Her last words were, "Sam, we love you."

Sam hung up the phone feeling very relieved that he made the call. He wished he had made it sooner but knew he had to do it when he was ready. He wasn't certain he would ever be ready. Somehow, it was his relationship with Arthur that had brought about this change in him. He was profoundly grateful.

Sam finished law school with honors. Everyone associated him with Arthur and had great respect for his legal expertise. He would be a formidable opponent in the courtroom.

The day Sam got word he had passed his Bar Exam, Arthur made preparations for a celebration. He invited a few of his closest associates, famous people in the field of law. It was an exceptional evening. Everyone seemed genuinely happy for both Arthur and Sam. They teased Sam that absolutely anyone could have become a successful attorney with Arthur as their mentor. Arthur beamed with pride. Sam felt humble and happy. There were several toasts made in their honor. It was a delightful evening.

Now it was time for Sam to join Arthur in his practice as a full time attorney. The rules of the game had changed. Sam had now taken on the responsibility of his profession. He knew he needed experience and knew he was in the right place with the right person to get it.

*****

Sam has taken some very large steps. He graduated law school, something he would never have believed was possible. In the process, he had formed a special relationship with Arthur.

The fact that Sam finally decided to share with someone his traumatic childhood experience was a very big step for him. He trusted Arthur, something that didn't come easily for him.

Sam was finally ready to confront that part of himself that had left the farm in an angry tirade. He was ready to acknowledge all of the love and care his aunt and uncle had shown him. He was ready to apologize. He was ready to face himself.

This was a critical juncture in Sam's life. He could have made very different choices. He could have clung to his anger and felt sorry for himself. He could have chosen to take it out on others. He could have made a miserable life for himself.

Sam's choices are to be commended. He made some very tough decisions under some very difficult circumstances. Somehow he had chosen to have a very positive focus. He had given his best to the opportunity

Arthur gave him, even though he really didn't have obvious skills at the time. Perhaps Arthur saw how hard he was trying and was determined to give him a break. Whatever it was, it worked.

Sam's life was now taking on a very positive direction. He was proud of what he had accomplished. He felt beyond blessed to have Arthur in his life. He knew he had a million things he didn't really believe he deserved.

Nonetheless, he had a grateful heart, and it showed.

CHAPTER FIVE

The Offer

After everyone had gone, Arthur and Sam moved to the study, sat down and had a serious conversation. Since Sam had reached his goal and was now an official attorney, he would want to start his practice. Arthur began asking him questions about how he envisioned his practice and which aspect of law did he want to turn into a speciality. Sam had to admit he really didn't know the answer to that question right now.

Sam and Arthur had not only concluded an employment agreement, they had managed to get Sam through law school. In addition, they had forged a very strong bond together. Arthur was about to go out on a very large limb. He asked Sam if he would like to enter into a legal partnership with him. Arthur was in his 70's now but his mind was still very sharp. Sam was stunned at such an offer. He knew that if word got out that Arthur was practicing again, in any capacity, they would have unimaginable work opportunities. They could also afford to be very selective.

This was a no-brainer question! Of course, Sam would jump at the chance to partner with Arthur. This was the offer of the century! They both understood, however, that Sam owed Arthur a year of his time as a result of graduating law school. After that, he felt ready to enter into a partnership with Arthur. It would be a total pleasure.

Over the next months, official word went around the world that Arthur and his associates were open for business. Quickly, the requests for their services came pouring in. Arthur and Sam spent many hours going through each of them before deciding on one or maybe two cases they would select. It was a tedious process. It was clear that all legal proceeds would go to Arthur. Sam was paying his dues.

The contract was signed for their first case. It was a homicide case of a highly-esteemed athletic figure. They would be the defense attorneys. They would be defending a 17 year old girl who was claiming self defense. They had their work cut out for them.

Sam was in awe of Arthur as they began to prepare their approach to the case. Sam could hardly keep up with him. He was brilliant. He came up with ideas Sam would never have considered.

It was clear to him how important personal experience was. Even though he was now a bona fide attorney, he had no experience. He was not ready for the big leagues. Arthur on the other hand was not only ready but enjoying the challenges of actually preparing a case and being in the courtroom again. It was almost fun to watch him work. What an incredible privilege to have this brilliant teacher in his life.

After numerous pretrial considerations, their first day in court would be tomorrow. The prosecuting attorney would lay out their case. They would also be giving their opening statement for the defense. It would be Sam's actual first performance in the courtroom. He was very nervous.

Sam and Arthur had gone over his opening remarks numerous times. Arthur tried to console Sam that he was not only ready to do this, but he would do it masterfully. Sam just looked at him and tilted his head.

The courtroom was filled to capacity. This was a very big case in the media. It was front and center. Of course, no one had ever even heard of Sam before. It was never more clear to him what a minor part he played on this team. Nonetheless this was his first opportunity to demonstrate his skills. He would do his absolute best.

Sam could hardly believe the prosecuting attorney. It was Natalie, the woman he met on the train several years ago. What a small world it was. She gave a very powerful opening statement. Sam's statement followed and was, at least, as powerful.

The trial lasted eight weeks. It was now in the hands of the jury. They had been deliberating for two days. Word had just come back that they had reached a decision. The jury was entering the courtroom and the verdict was about to be read. Arthur turned to Sam and said, "No matter, Sam. We did our best." Their client was acquitted! Sam had never felt more relieved in his life.

Sam and Arthur took a month off before diving into their next case. It was a case of a hit and run of a child. Their client swore he was not guilty. They met with their proposed client. They agreed they did not wish to defend him. The child was paralyzed for life and the man did not have a strong alibi. They decided to pass. Sam realized that if he were practicing alone, he would not have had the privilege of turning down people he didn't want to defend. He was beginning to feel Arthur was about the best thing that ever happened to him.

Over the next few years, Arthur and Sam tried several cases and never lost a single one. This was worth a gold mine to Sam as an attorney. His reputation grew and clients were seeking him as their attorney. This was very gratifying for him but he knew he owed it all to Arthur.

One morning at 3AM an alarm sounded in the house. Sam knew this meant some kind of serious emergency. He jumped out of bed, grabbed his robe and headed down the hallway. He raced to Arthur's room. He found him face down on the floor beside his bed. Sam turned him over. He wasn't breathing. Sam dialed 911 and began giving CPR. Within minutes, the paramedics arrived and administered life saving efforts. It was useless. He was pronounced dead. Sam felt as though his whole world had just caved in. He remembered these horrible violent feelings of death and despair. He watched as the paramedics covered his face. Sam left the room in tears. What now? The greatest strength of his life was gone. He felt five years old again as though he was reliving his traumatic childhood memories.

Arthur and Sam had never discussed his last will and testament. He had no clue. He didn't even know who Arthur's attorney was or who even had a copy of it. Who would make the funeral arrangements? He had a million questions and didn't have a clue who to ask. Right now, he was simply caught up in his own personal grief and didn't want to have to think like a lawyer. He spent the next thirty minutes in the shower. When he came out, he crashed on his bed and was sound asleep when his phone rang.

The call was from Stephen, one of Arthur's attorney friends he had invited to Sam's celebration party. He asked Sam if he had some time that day to meet with him. Sam had slept until 11 a.m. He could hardly believe it was that late. They agreed to meet at 1 p.m. in Arthur's study.

Right on time, Stephen was at the house for their meeting. Stephen said he would simply cut to the chase. He said he was the executor of Arthur's will. He said there would be no formal reading of it but he wanted to personally share it with Sam. He handed him a copy.

Sam took it from the envelope and began reading. He sat down and simply looked at Stephen. Arthur bequeathed all of his assets to support a charitable foundation. He had designated Charlie and Stephen to be the co-administrators of the estate. He had discussed the details with Stephen. It would require a lot of research, planning and development.

Stephen explained that all of the funeral arrangements were already made. He didn't need to worry about anything. Arthur had planned everything meticulously before he passed. He did not want to place any burdens on Sam. Along with the will, Stephen handed Sam a sealed envelope with his name on it. That evening, he opened it.

Sam,

What a delight it has been to mentor you. I'm proud of you.

I know that you and Stephen can be trusted with my portfolio. I entrust it all to you knowing in confidence that you will use my assets wisely and well. Make me proud,

My deepest thanks to you for being the person you are. I believe God has always had His hand on your life. Trust Him, Sam.

Arthur

This man knew Sam better than anyone. Sam didn't take these words lightly. He would always keep this letter and take his words to heart. He had so much to think about now. He was glad they had no pending cases. He was free to take as much time as he needed to process all of these events in his life. Right now, he simply felt overwhelmed.

The memorial service and burial were almost more than Sam could handle. He had never buried anyone he loved this much. What an incredible gift he had been in Sam's life. Sam was the last one to leave the cemetery. It was a beautiful service. The church was full. It was a beautiful tribute to his life. What a send off! How privileged Charlie had been to have known such a man.

That night, Sam found himself sitting outside by the pool, sipping a drink he used to have with Arthur. Arthur could not have been more present than if we were sitting right there with him. Sam could feel his presence. Sam was certain he would always feel his presence, especially in the courtroom.

All of Arthur's staff had been relieved of their duties. They were no longer needed. Arthur had compensated each of them monetarily and had given each a personal note of gratitude for their services. For all of his brilliance, he didn't have an arrogant bone in his body. What a role model he was.

The next day, Sam contacted Stephen. They set up a weekly schedule to begin fulfilling Arthur's wishes for a foundation to be established. They agreed it would be called the Arthur Adams Foundation. Sam felt proud as he said it. They had a name for the Foundation.

Sam and Stephen agreed that this would be a good time for them to step back and give serious reflection as to what kind of foundation they should establish. They both had research and a lot of thinking to do in preparation for how this might all come together. They agreed to meet again in one month. They had a lot to discuss.

*****

Just when Sam was beginning to feel solid ground under his feet, his world collapsed, yet again! Arthur had given him an incredible beginning to his career. He was his coach and mentor. He showed him how to win cases.

He taught him how to be a successful attorney and a better person. Sam could never have had a better teacher. The reality now was that Arthur was no longer a daily part of Sam's life nor would he ever be again.

Sam had known a lot of loss in his young life. It was the weakest part of him. He never understood how to let go. He never wanted to have to let go -- of his family, or of Arthur.

At the same time, Sam realized what an incredible gift he had been given . Arthur gave him a career, a relationship and showed him a kind of love he had never experienced before. Arthur was the greatest gift of his life.

Sam was determined to partner with Stephen and find a way to make Arthur proud. He would give all of his energy to making the best use of his assets. They would figure out the best possible foundation and set it all in motion. He was confident. He was excited to make it happen. It would be a special way that he could communicate his gratitude for all that Arthur had done for him.

Sam had found a way to frame Arthur's passing that allowed him to stay positive and motivated. Already, he had formulated the name of the foundation: The Arthur Adams Foundation. It was simple and perfect. It was kind of the way he felt about Arthur post-mortem.

CHAPTER 6

Mending Fences

Sam decided this would be the right time for him to make a trip back to the farm to visit his aunt. He needed to get away and give himself some time in a different environment in order to see things more clearly. He made arrangements with a trusted caretaker to look after the house while he was away. He planned to leave the following morning.

He thought about contacting his aunt to let her know he was coming but decided against it. He would simply show up.

The next morning Sam boarded a train to take him back to the farm. He would be returning as a very different person than the one he was when he lived there. This would be a powerful experience for him. He was certain of that. He hoped he was ready.

He enjoyed sitting in the dome car watching all of the beautiful scenery. Part of him felt as though he was really seeing it for the first time. He had more drinks than usual. In a million years, he could never have envisioned his life taking these turns. He couldn't get his brain around it. He had no idea which direction his life would go from here. Actually, these were the same feelings he had the last time he rode the train, although for very different reasons.

Finally, it was his stop. With some fear and trepidation, he took a deep breath, grabbed his bag and stepped off of the train. It was a few miles to the farm. He would catch a cab.

By the time he reached the farm, it was late afternoon. He was overcome with emotion as he walked up the steps to the house. The last time he was there was his graduation day. What a horrible memory that was.

The front door was open. Sam knocked on the screen door and waited for his aunt to answer. When she came to the door and saw Sam, she flung it open and wrapped her arms around him. They were both overcome with emotion. She wept convulsively. Sam simply held her and said nothing. After several minutes, they went into the house and were seated at the kitchen table.

They both had a million questions. They talked for several hours. They ate a sandwich together. Then, Sam went out to the barn to visit Zipper. He was still alive. Sam had nothing but happy memories of his time with this little pony. He had been a very special friend to him at a time when he needed it most. It was great to see him. He walked around the farm and took in all of the good memories of his time there. He realized more than ever how hard his aunt's whole family had worked to make Sam feel like part of the family. He also noticed how many things were in disrepair.

Perhaps if Sam hadn't already experienced so much pain in his young life, he could have handled the lie about his father's death better than he did. He realized he couldn't go back and redo that part of his life. That bell had already rung. It simply was what it was. He needed to let it go and try to create something positive. He needed to learn the lesson and commit to healing and creating new positive memories.

Sam decided to spend the week with his aunt. There were a lot of things that needed fixing and repair. He would love to help her. This was as therapeutic for him as it was for her. As the week wore on, they shared more and more of their lives. By the end of the week, there were genuine and loving feelings between them.

They both apologized profusely to one another for things in their past. It was important to Sam that his aunt really understood when he expressed his gratitude for all they had done for him. He wasn't sure where he would be now if they hadn't helped him. They were a special gift to him. He wanted to be certain she understood that.

He mended the fence, fixed the porch, repaired the steps and painted the shed. He made it a point everyday to spend time with Zipper. It was a way of reconnecting with his boyhood days.. Also, he planned to take his teddy bear with him when he left. There were still a lot of little boy in him.

The last evening there, he took his aunt out to dinner. They went to a very nice restaurant where they met up with one of her daughters. What a delightful visit they did have. Sam was so grateful he had made the trip. He was feeling very relaxed. At dinner, Sam glanced at his aunt and, just for a second, saw his mother. He had never really noticed the similarity before, even though they were twins. It gave him a warm feeling.

As they drove back to the farm, they had some lighter moments and enjoyed some genuine laughter. Sam remembered the time his aunt painted the toilet seat and forgot to tell George. It took him an hour to get himself off of it and there was a ring of dark hairs all around it. Everyone thought it was hilarious except for George, of course.

His aunt prepared his favorite breakfast. It was time for Sam to leave to catch the train. He took his aunt's hands in his and expressed his genuine appreciation of his time with her. He said he would cherish it. Things could not have gone better on this visit. It was just what they both needed.

As Sam walked out the door, his aunt reached out her hand and said that she and his uncle George wanted him to have this. It was a beautiful ring George had worn for most of his life. It was given to him by his grandmother and had been worn by his grandfather. His initials were inscribed in the gold inside the band. It was a beautiful emerald, surrounded by diamonds. It had been appraised at thousands of dollars. Sam was honored. He put it on his finger, kissed her on the cheek and climbed into his taxi.

Back on the train, Sam was, once again, sitting in the dome car drinking in the scenery and his rum and coke. The world looked brighter and more beautiful. He was brighter.

Sam was 29 years old, a lawyer who had gotten off to a very good start. He lived in a mansion (that didn't belong to him) and had more 'stuff' than he could ever have imagined. How had he gone from being a five year old who survived a violent crash to being a practicing attorney? He could never have imagined it. However, now was a critical point in his life where he needed to really come to terms with what he wanted his life to be. Enough of trauma, violence and betrayal. Those were things he didn't want. What did he want? That was the critical question. He had more questions than answers.

Seattle was two hours away. Sam had contacted the caretaker of the estate to let him know he would be arriving today. Now that he was back, he had a million nagging details with which to attend. Right now, he just wanted to be left alone until he felt like dealing with all of the issues he needed to solve. Even though he was physically rested, he was emotionally exhausted. He needed time.

When Sam arrived back at the estate, there were at least a million issues that needed tending. Just sorting through the mail was exhausting. There were several requests for legal counsel. Some of them looked interesting but Sam knew he couldn't handle those pressures right now. First he had to get together with himself.

That Sunday, Sam went to church, mostly out of habit. He knew it would be what he would be doing if Arthur was still alive. The sermon was on finding direction in one's life. The pastor used the scripture: "Trust in the Lord with all your heart and lean not unto your own understanding. In all your ways acknowledge Him and He will direct your path." He had heard these scriptures from Proverbs before. They were some of Arthur's favorite verses. He pondered them as he drove home.

Sundays were hard for Sam. He remembered them as a day for family time. He had fond memories of fun times on Sunday. They always had a special meal to enjoy. He really missed those special family times. He was alone and lonely. Maybe that was one of the first things in his life he needed to fix. He had been so busy working for Arthur and getting his education that he had done little socializing. Maybe it was time to change that.

He hardly knew where to begin. He knew he didn't want to join a dating site on the internet. It crossed his mind to wonder if this is what Arthur experienced. He indicated he kind of had it all but there was an important piece missing in his life. Sam felt the same way. Maybe he should advertise in the newspaper for an assistant, just as Arthur had done. That thought made him laugh out loud.

In the days and weeks that followed, Sam was able to accomplish most of the details that required his attention. He was still behind in his correspondence but had made some headway.. Among the 'junk' mail he received was an invitation to a church social. It was actually a fundraiser to benefit needy children.

Sam set it aside. Ironically, he received a phone call the following day with a personal invitation to attend the fundraiser. In a weak moment, he agreed to attend. It was being held at Arthur's church.

Sam decided to attend the dinner. He went an hour early to take part in the silent auction. There were actually some very nice items on which to bid. As he was posting a bid, he felt someone bump into him. As he turned around, he recognized her. It was Natalie, the girl he had met on the train and had seen once in the courtroom. She looked very nice. Sam smiled at her.

She told him he looked familiar and asked if they had met before. Sam reminded her of their breakfast together on the train. She remembered immediately and said she was embarrassed.

It was almost time for the dinner to begin. They walked into the dining room together and chose the same table. Actually, it was kind of nice for Sam to bump into someone he had met before.

The event was well intended and seemed to be a cut above what Sam had expected. It was a lovely catered meal. The people at their table were very pleasant. It felt good to Sam and he was glad he had chosen to come.

There was a brief presentation by a psychologist who worked with traumatized and abused children. Sam was sensitive to what she had to say and identified with her description of traumatized children. He knew those feelings up close and personal. It was his story she was telling.

It was shortly after that when people were invited to place their gifts in the envelope next to their plate. They were to be collected soon. Sam got out his checkbook and wrote a check for $1,000.00. He knew it was for a good cause. He also knew that Arthur would have more than approved.

As the silent auction results were revealed, Sam had won a dinner for two at an exclusive restaurant. He was pleased to get it. Almost without thinking, he turned to Natalie and explained that he had no one to share dinner with and invited her to join him. She smiled and accepted. They exchanged phone numbers. It had been a good evening. He drove home in higher spirits than when he arrived. He slept well that night.

Tomorrow, Sam and Stephen would be meeting to discuss Arthur's endowment. It was time for them to come up with a plan. Sam was beginning to give serious thought to making the foundation include family law. He thought this would have pleased Arthur. Stephen agreed. They had a lot to talk about.

*****

Sam was a compassionate man. It was what guided him into his decision to right the wrong of his disregard and disrespect for his aunt and uncle. He knew it was what he knew he needed to do in order to finish up his painful unfinished business. Sam was sincerely sorry for the way he handled his anger. It actually helped him understand better what his aunt and uncle had felt when they lied to him. Everyone makes difficult choices they wish they could take back. Unfortunately, that is not the shape of life. It is part of the crooked path.

Sam experienced a kind of peace in his life even while he was grieving over the loss of Arthur. Perhaps it was because of his relationship with Arthur that he really wanted to come back and make things right with his family. He was sorry his uncle had passed. The love he and his aunt had for each other had never been more real to him.

Arthur's passing helped Sam to understand that he was ready for the next chapter in his life. He had reached his goal of becoming an attorney. Arthur had passed. Besides his practice and the work of creating the Arthur Adams Foundation, Sam knew he needed something more in his life. He was ready to find a relationship.

Arthur's church felt like a safe place for Sam to go. Perhaps it was a bit of fate that took him there the night he got reacquainted with Natalie. This would be a life-changing event for him. It would be the beginning of his first bonding experience with a woman. Unfortunately, it would not be the first recurring trauma in Sam's life.

None of us know whose path will intersect our own and what impact it may have on us. Sometimes we are greatly surprised. Sometimes we are surprised by joy, sometimes by grief.

It is all part of our crooked path.

CHAPTER 7

Natalie

The next day he called Natalie and made a dinner date. He would pick her up at 7:30 p.m. for an 8 p m dinner. She lived alone in a nice townhouse. She was wearing a lovely black dress and jewelry. Her hair was up in a twist and she looked quite stunning. In fact, he was surprised at how striking she was.

The restaurant was exquisite. They had a lovely table overlooking the water. It was perfect. They were both attorneys and travelled in similar circles. However, tonight would not be about their work. Their mood was light and pleasant. Neither of them shared a lot of personal information about themselves. However, Natalie did share that she had lost her parents at an early age and was raised by her grandparents. She was so young when it happened that she didn't remember them. In some ways, that had made it easier for her.

Perhaps they had both been drawn to the church dinner because it was a fundraiser for children. Both of them knew about childhood trauma. Sam was realizing that they had some important things in common. That felt good to him.

The evening passed very quickly and both Sam and Natalie seemed quite comfortable with one another. On the way home, Natalie told Sam about a church social that was being held on Saturday night. She said she planned to go and invited him. They would go bowling. She said she wasn't a very good bowler but enjoyed the people in the group. He walked her to the door, took her hand and told her he had really enjoyed the evening. She thanked him and said she would see him on Saturday.

Sam woke the next morning feeling better than usual. He had enjoyed himself with Natalie and looked forward to seeing her again. He had never had a close relationship with a woman before. It felt good to be with someone with a similar world view. He looked forward to getting to know her better.

Sam and Natalie had a great time at the bowling party. Sam was enjoying getting to know some new people. It also motivated him to attend church on Sunday. He ran into people he knew. They had breakfast together afterward. There were some very impressive people in that group. They were well educated but not arrogant. He liked that about them. That was similar to how he saw himself.

The more time he spent with Natalie, the more he liked her. She seemed to have a depth to her and a spirit of compassion which made her character come alive. It reminded him a little of how he remembered his own mother. She was starting to matter to him. This scared him a little.

Sam and Natalie began seeing each other on a regular basis. Their conversations were becoming more personal.

Sam felt it was just a matter of time before he was going to have to disclose more things about himself to her. He was way out of his comfort zone although part of him really wanted her to know who he really was.

One evening his phone rang. It was Ned from the singles group of the church. He said he had just heard that Natalie had been hit head-on by a drunk driver and had been transported to the hospital by an ambulance. He told Sam the name of the hospital.

Sam raced to his car and drove to the hospital. He went immediately to the emergency section and asked about her. He was told she was in surgery. Because he wasn't family they wouldn't disclose any further information. They said he was welcome to wait and they would keep him informed when she was out of surgery.

Sam waited. As he sat there, he felt his whole life flashed before his eyes. What was there about trauma and death that seemed to follow him around?

This was one of the few times in Sam's life that he had ever prayed for anyone. He asked God to please let Natalie live. He actually begged Him for her life. His eyes filled with tears. He could hardly believe his own emotion.

After what seemed like a lifetime, an emergency room nurse approached Sam and asked why he was there. He shared that Natalie was out of surgery and had been transferred to the intensive care unit. He wished he knew someone in her family to call. Perhaps he could call back the guy who told him about the accident. Maybe he would know someone close to her who would know who to call.

Actually, as he was leaving the emergency area of the hospital, he spotted several of the people from the singles group who had come there. He told them she was out of surgery and in the ICU. They invited Sam to join them in a prayer on Natalie's behalf.

After that, they went to the intensive care unit and inquired about her. Again, the nurse asked if they were family. When she learned none of them were, she told them she was in critical condition and they would know more in the morning. Sam's heart sank. Those were words he didn't want to hear. They all decided to wait together.

Someone made a run to Starbucks and brought back coffee for everyone. The four of them talked quietly as they waited. Some of them shared traumatic experiences they had in their lives. There was a quiet sense of caring which permeated their conversation. It was clear these people believed that God held the keys to life and death. He was the One who decided who lived and who died. Natalie's life was in His hands and they prayed for His will to be done. Sam didn't feel quite as trusting. He wanted Natalie to live, end of story.

The night passed quickly. Some of them fell asleep for a few hours. Sam was awake the entire time. A little after 9AM, an ICU nurse approached them. They said Natalie had survived the night. Her stats were mostly stable. She would remain in intensive care indefinitely for now.

The group left and went home. None of them knew any of Natalie's family. No one was certain if her grandparents were still alive. Someone was going to check with the law firm where she worked and see if they had any information. Clearly, people were very concerned for and cared about her. This was a very difficult day for Sam.

Sam took a 30 minute shower and climbed into bed for some much-needed sleep. He tossed and turned, thinking about Natalie and wondering if he would ever see her again.

Around 5 p.m., the phone rang. It was Ned from the singles group at church. He had been at the hospital last night. He called to say that there had been no changes in Natalie's condition. He asked Sam if they could get together. He said he wanted to talk to him although he didn't say what about. Sam agreed to meet him at 6PM at a place that made good burgers and fries.

Ned was a handsome guy. He was a CPA. He seemed to be a popular guy. Ned asked Sam if he could speak candidly. Sam was taken back by this remark but assured Ned he could say whatever he needed to say.

Ned said that he wanted Sam to feel he could be himself when he was with them. They respected his work as an attorney and the relationship he had formed with Arthur. Everyone loved Arthur who spoke so highly of Sam. Now that Arthur was gone, they were hoping to feel as close to him as they did to Arthur. Ned told Sam he just decided to share this information in hopes of making things easier for Sam. They held direct eye-contact and Sam nodded.

Ned said he brought a book he wanted to give to Sam to read. It was one of his favorites. He said he had no idea what Sam's spiritual beliefs were and that he simply wanted to share a book that had meant a lot to him and had a strong impact on his spiritual beliefs. The book was by C.S. Lewis, <u>Mere Christianity.</u>

Sam thanked him for the book and said he would read it. Besides that, Sam was stunned. He had been so careful to try to hide his true identity. He felt a bit intimidated now and a little bit ashamed. Why did he feel he needed to hide?

Ned and his group were offering Sam genuine friendship which is what he was really seeking. He was, apparently, making it harder than it had to be. In his own way, Arthur had been trying to pave the way for him. Some part of him felt relieved. This was an unexpected opportunity to make some friends and maybe find a new direction in his life.

As they left the restaurant, they shook hands and Sam thanked him. He said he looked forward to getting to know everyone better. How could Sam possibly feel betrayed by Arthur who had nothing but his best interests at heart? Sam decided this was all for the best. He would move forward and see where it took him.

As they were leaving, they both agreed to visit the hospital again tomorrow and check on Natalie's condition. So far, no one even knew the extent of her injuries or whether any family of hers had been contacted. There were far more questions than answers.

As Sam was driving home, he remembered that Natalie had a little dog. He wondered whether or not anyone else knew this or was taking care of him. He decided to drive to her house.

The front door was locked. He went to the rear of the house and peeked in the kitchen window. He saw the little dog laying next to his empty food bowl and no water. The door was locked. He decided to break the bottom window pane. He unlocked the door, scooped the little dog into his arms. He was shaking. Sam grabbed a bag of his food he found under the counter, grabbed his dishes and took him home with him.

He named the little dog, "Max." He had no idea what his real name was. He devoured a bowl of food and drank endlessly. He was starved and dehydrated. Sam was so glad he found him in time. Actually, Sam rather liked having a little fur baby in the house. He turned Max loose in the backyard. He would have more than an acre to run around. He would keep his food and water bowl outside. Max seemed happy to be there.

That night, Sam brought Max up to his bedroom and let him spend the night on the bed. He gave Max his teddy bear to snuggle. Poor little Max had been locked up in that house for nearly 4 days by himself. Sam had likely just saved his life. How he wished he could do the same for Natalie!

The next day at the hospital, Sam made a special effort to see if he could gather some specific information about Natalie. He identified himself as an attorney, said he was a close personal friend of Natalie's. He added that she had no family they could locate. He pleaded for anything they could tell him.

The nurse motioned to him to walk with her down the corridor. She said they had nearly lost Natalie the day before. She was in a coma with severe neurological trauma. She also told him she had the best neurologist in the hospital treating her. She was in good hands.

While Sam was pleased at gaining a little more information, he was very troubled by her diagnosis. It wasn't looking good. Even if she did recover, it would likely be a very long rehabilitation process. He wondered if it was even possible to have a full recovery given her traumatic injuries. Time would tell.

As Sam was leaving the hospital, he ran into Ned and his friends. He shared with them the information the nurse had given him about Natalie. No one said a word.

He shared with all of them that he had Natalie's dog. He had since contacted a window repair company to come and replace the pane he had broken. Some of them knew she had a dog but no one had thought to go to her house and check on him. They were relieved and thanked Sam.

As the weeks went by, Natalie's condition went unchanged. The prayer group had continued faithfully. In the meantime, Sam and little Max were beginning to bond. Sam had bought him a ball and spent time playing with him every day. He continued to sleep on Sam's bed at night. Sam was beginning to really enjoy his company. He didn't feel quite as alone. Sam was beginning to realize just how much he missed Arthur.

One day, while Sam was looking for a book in Arthur's study, he came across a copy of C.S. Lewis' Mere Christianity. He had forgotten all about the copy Ned had given him. It was still in the glove compartment of his car. He went out to his car and retrieved it. That night, he started reading it.

He was very surprised to understand that Lewis was an Oxford scholar and a devout atheist. Like Sam, he had lost his mother as a young boy and was sent off to boarding school at the age of nine. He had a very difficult childhood. Sam was surprised that he was identifying with Lewis. This challenged him to continue reading. Before he knew it, he had devoured the whole book. He couldn't put it down.

Lewis had gone from being a hardened atheist to being a devout Christian. It would take time for him to digest the life of C.S. Lewis. It inspired him to read other books by C.S. Lewis. Eventually, he rented the movie Shadowlands, the story of Lewis' life.

Slowly, he was beginning to digest and understand the process of Lewis' choices that took him down a very different path than the one he was on. Perhaps this was also possible for Sam. He wasn't at all certain, but he was open. For now, that felt like enough.

In the fifth week of Natalie's time in the intensive care unit, she became conscious. She had no memory of the accident and no sense of time. She was shocked to hear it had been five weeks since the crash. The first thing she asked about was her dog.

Her doctor explained that he didn't know about her dog but he mentioned that she had a very faithful group of friends who came to the hospital on a daily basis to check on her. He was not aware of any family visitation. He asked the nurse to inquire about the dog and inform Natalie. She was thrilled to learn her furry friend was being well cared for by Sam. It made her smile.

The next week, Natalie was transferred from the ICU to a regular bed in the hospital. Now her friends could visit. Sam surprised her by gaining special permission to bring little Max to the hospital for a visit. Natalie was thrilled to see him. They cuddled for a long time. She thanked Sam profusely for looking after him.

While it was great news that Natalie was out of her coma, conscious and her memory had returned, she was paralyzed from the waist down. Her doctor was uncertain if she would ever regain feeling in that part of her body. For now, she was confined to a wheelchair. Her days were spent in the rehabilitation unit of the hospital. As the days and weeks passed, her spirits became dark and she seriously wondered if she would ever walk again.

She let her friends know that she thought it best if they only came weekly or even monthly. She was very depressed and it was stressful for her to be around others.

In truth, she really didn't want to see anybody, not even little Max. She was actually starting to regret that she had ever survived the crash. She was giving up.

It was nearly midnight when Sam's phone rang. He had been sound asleep with little Max at the foot of the bed. It was Ned. He apologized for the late hour. He said he had some very disturbing news to give him.

The nurse had found Natalie unresponsive in her bed. She had hoarded her sleeping meds for a week and had taken them all at one time. She was dead. She had left an envelope, addressed to Sam. The hospital was requesting he come and get it.

Sam hung up the phone, sat on the edge of the bed and placed his hands over his face. How much more loss could he take? Why did she do it?

Slowly he got dressed, grabbed his keys and headed for the hospital. He went to the floor where she had been and checked with the nurse. She handed him the envelope with his name on it. He shoved it into his jacket pocket and left the hospital.

When he got home, he went into Arthur's study and sat down in his chair. Somehow it was the most stable place he could think of. He was dreading reading Natalie's letter.

It read:

Sam,

I don't even feel worthy of asking forgiveness from anyone for the horrible thing I have done. I am so sorry. I just couldn't find the strength to face another day. I would never have believed I could feel this way. I have enclosed my last will and testament. From one attorney to another, I know you will know how to honor it. My deepest thanks to you for caring for my precious little, "Max." He is in loving hands and I can't thank you enough for saving his life.

You are a very special man, Sam. I secretly wished that someday we might have made a commitment to spend the rest of our lives together. I guess it wasn't meant to be.

My love,

Natalie

With tears in his eyes, Sam opened and read the will. She had left everything to Sam. She expressed an interest that since he really didn't need the money that he would donate it to an organization that supported needy, traumatized and abused children. She was sure he would find just the right place.

Her townhouse was fully paid for. She had a life insurance policy for another $100,000.00 and he was the beneficiary. She also owned stocks and bonds with an impressive portfolio. She had done very well for herself. It crossed Charlie's mind to wonder if this money should be merged with Arthurs and put into a foundation for helping children. He would run this idea by Stephen when he saw him.

Sam went to church the following Sunday. The sermon was on "Undergoing what we don't understand." It was timely. Only God knows and understands the hearts and minds of each of His creations. The scripture was: "A man's steps are ordered of the Lord. How, then, can a man understand his own way?" Sam, nor anyone else, had walked in Natalie's shoes. No one had a right to judge her. Only God knew her heart and understood her choices. End of story.

Over the next months, Sam began accepting new cases and spent long days preparing for numerous trials. He felt the presence of Arthur every step of the way. Actually, he talked to him out loud sometimes when he was in the study, preparing his opening statements. The study had become his favorite room in the house. Arthur was there and fully present to give his input on anything Sam wished to discuss. He was always the elephant in the room.

Sam was surprised at how comfortable he felt in the courtroom. He emulated Arthur in so many ways. He would always be extremely grateful for his influence in his life. He felt it everyday.

Now that his calendar was no longer filled, Sam and Stephen had time to begin making some decisions regarding the Foundation. As it turned out, Stephen thought his idea of creating a facility where legal expertise and family law could merge might be an excellent idea for Arthur's foundation.

Sam informed Stephen he was headed to a conference in London on this very topic. He also informed him about Natalie's will and since she was so devoted to helping children, he was thinking seriously of adding her funds to the Arthur Adams Foundation. Stephen liked the idea.

Sam hoped he would be returning from the conference in London with fresh ideas and new found understanding of family law. He and Stephen formulated a new schedule which each of them recorded in their daytimers. They both realized this was going to take a great deal of their time and energy.

*****

Sam was absolutely traumatized by yet another suicide. He was weary of losing people in his life. It almost felt like a curse of some kind. He wanted to put a sign on his heart that said, "Closed!"

Sam felt overwhelmed by his grief over Arthur and Natalie. Part of him felt angry at all of the loss in his life. Right now, he would simply focus on his work and on developing the Arthur Adams Foundation. This seemed to be a safe place to put his energies for now.

Sam cherished little Max. He had become his very special little furry friend. He greeted Sam each day with yelps and sloppy kisses. He was always so excited to see him. Sam felt safe with Max.

CHAPTER 8

London

On Saturday, Sam and Max were in the study and Sam was cleaning up the weekly correspondence. Sam was leaving the following day for the conference in London involving children and the law.

Although Sam had a heart for helping children, he had never actually taken on any legal case involving children. Maybe it was time to expand his practice. He hadn't really given much thought to children's needs since he contemplated the best place to bequeath the donation from Natalie's estate to a Christian charity devoted to helping children. He was still pondering that idea and hoped the conference would help guide his decision.

Sam was trying to decide how to best arrange for Max's care while he was away in London. He contacted Ned. They hadn't spoken in many months, actually since Natalie's memorial service. Sam explained that he was headed to a conference and needed someone to look after Max for a week. Without hesitation, Ned agreed and said he would be happy to look after the little guy. Sam suggested maybe Ned would be willing to live in his house for a week so that Max could stay in familiar territory. Ned agreed.

Sam was finishing up his packing and had an early flight the next morning to London. He had never been there before and was looking forward to the trip. He and Max had taken their run that day. He fed Max a special treat that night. He would miss the little guy.

Sam barely made his flight. It was full. He had an aisle seat at the rear of the plane. The seat beside him was empty. He had brought C.S. Lewis' book <u>Mere Christianity</u> to read on the plane. It had been quite awhile since he had read it and he wanted to review it and give serious thought to it at a time where he knew he would not be interrupted.

He was struck with the same thoughts as before. He identified with Lewis' deep wound of losing his mother, having a difficult childhood but finding a way to keep going and achieve some difficult accomplishments. The overshadowing theme of loss and faith is what attracted him to this book. It was one of the biggest challenges in his life.

It was a pleasant flight. They were preparing for landing. The weather in London was at least ten degrees cooler than Seattle. He retrieved his luggage, hailed a taxi and arrived at the hotel where the conference was being held.

He immediately fell in love with the British accent. It seemed to have a gentleness to it that resonated with Sam. He was impressed with London and with the hotel. He soon got used to drinking tea and eating scones. His room was lovely, overlooking a courtyard. It felt good to be there. He had a bit of jet lag and realized he needed some sleep.

Sam slept soundly. His alarm sounded at 6AM. He showered and found a nice place in the hotel to sit and eat his breakfast. He decided to read the British newspaper and found it interesting. He enjoyed reading the classified ads. No one was looking for a 'junior assistant.' It made him smile.

Sam was one of the first to register for the conference. It was attended by more than 200 people. The schedule looked impressive. He was looking forward to it. He wished Arthur was there to join him. Somehow Sam always felt the presence of Arthur.

After the conference was introduced, the first speaker was a sitting judge from the United States Supreme Court. This was more than Sam had expected. The judge shared some startling and depressing statistics about children around the world. The law had provided rules for the treatment of animals before it had made legal provisions for the rights of children.

Runaways and children living on the streets have become a new normal. Child neglect, endangerment, abuse and homelessness have become a way of life. A high percentage of children in the world are going to sleep hungry. Many die of starvation. Many suffer mental illness from years of abuse. The foster care system remains overwhelmed.

It was a very powerful beginning, to say the least. They had just received a very graphic description of children and the law, in their faces.

The next two speakers presented specific cases they had either defended or prosecuted. They had graphic details that were hard to hear. Most prosecutable crimes of child abuse were never even brought to trial. Children were threatened and refused to testify, often against their own parents.

When they broke for lunch, Sam returned to his room, turned on the TV and grabbed a beer from the mini-fridge in his room. The morning had been intense. He needed a break.

The afternoon presentations were less graphic and intense and focused more on specific legal principles that were effective in prosecuting cases. This interested Sam a great deal. He took copious notes.

When the conference was over for the day, Sam felt exhausted. He purchased a sandwich from the cafe, took it to his room, turned on the TV and got lost in one of his favorite shows. He was hoping tomorrow would be less intense.

By the last day of the conference, Sam had a pile of handouts he had received from the various speakers and believed them to be valuable in understanding and managing actual legal cases involving children. He was realizing how little he actually knew about case law in this particular venue.

Because everyone was wearing a name tag which identified where they were from, people were aware of Sam's origins. Right after the last presentation, Sam was approached by a young woman who asked him if he had known Arthur. He was totally taken back by the question.

She said she asked because he and Sam were both attorneys from the same city. One of her colleagues had been in law school at the same time as Arthur and couldn't say enough good things about him. Arthur was quoted a lot in their law firm. He seemed to represent the final authority on legal protocol.

This woman's name was Allison. She was from San Francisco. She looked to be about Sam's same age. She had a very pretty face and long, flowing blonde hair. There was a softness to her which attracted Sam.

Sam responded by telling her that he did, indeed, know Arthur, that he had been his mentor and business associate. He said Arthur had been about the best thing that had ever happened to him in his whole life.

Allison smiled at Sam. She invited him to have a drink with her. Sam had nothing else to do. He decided to join her. Sitting across from her at a table in the hotel bar caused him to notice just how beautiful she really was. He asked her about her law practice.

She told Sam she had been a practicing attorney for five years and that her law firm specialized in prosecuting child offenders. This interested Sam very much. He asked her to tell him more. She responded for the next two hours, explaining to Sam why she felt this was her calling.

She had been the victim of serious abuse as a child. Her perpetrator had been sentenced to life in prison. Sam could only imagine the intensity of the crime to have received such a sentence.

She was telling him a lot about herself without the details. This impressed him. He was careful not to be invasive by asking her any pressing questions. He simply accepted why she devoted her legal energies to prosecuting child offenders. No wonder she had attended this conference. Sam had just gained enormous respect for her passion and compassion for using her energies for good, to fight evil she had experienced personally. Sam liked this woman!

The subject turned back to Arthur. Allison was telling Sam some of the specific contributions Arthur had made to their practice, totally unbeknown to him. Sam listened intently and most of it made him smile. He had learned these same truths from Arthur himself.

Sam inquired of Allison if she had ever heard of an attorney named Natalie Williams? Allison dropped her head and said that she did know Natalie and was extremely troubled by her passing.

Sam continued to tell Allison of the tremendous financial contribution she had made to helping children. He gave some detail and even told her the amount. She was beyond impressed. She seemed to have genuine regard and respect for Natalie. She had nothing but positive things to say about her.

Sam even told Allison about little Max and what a sweet companion he had become. Allison smiled. She commented that Natalie and Sam must have had a close relationship if he now had her dog. Sam smiled. He wasn't ready to share any additional details.

After three hours of very pleasant conversation, Allison said she still needed to pack and had an early flight the next morning. Sam shared that he, too, had an early flight. As it turned out, they were booked on the same flight. Sam was flying into San Francisco, then catching a flight to Seattle. This was ironic. At that moment, in his mind's eye, he could see Arthur smiling.

They exchanged cell phone numbers and parted for the evening. The next morning they were both up early and at the gate, ready to board their plane back to America. Sam spotted her in the terminal. On the way there, he passed a Starbucks, purchased two coffees and made his way to the gate. He approached her and offered her the coffee. She smiled at him and graciously accepted.

They agreed they would like to be seated next to one another on the flight back to San Francisco. It seemed they might have a lot to talk about. They boarded the flight and were comfortably in their seats. In what seemed like a simple hour, they were preparing for landing. Their conversation flowed effortlessly. They shared happy and sad events, legal issues, case law and family memories. Nothing seemed off base. Sam actually disclosed more to her than he had intended. She did the same. They seemed to have a strong sense of comfort with one another. This came as a real surprise to both of them.

After they landed and Allison collected her luggage, it was time for her to catch a cab and head home. Sam was at a loss for words (which was not like him at all). He told Allison that it was a complete and unexpected pleasure to meet her. He thanked her for approaching him and inviting contact.

Sam made a special point to Allison that if there was ever any way in which he could help her or her firm with legal expertise for a case they were working on to always feel more than free to call on him. He would only be too happy to help. Allison smiled, gave him a gentle hug and a sweet kiss on his cheek. He watched her get into a taxi and disappear. He was at a loss for words.

On the flight to Seattle, Sam's head was filled with recalling the long conversation he had just had with Allison. He couldn't recall ever having such a conversation with anyone except for maybe Arthur. Allison was an amazing woman. She was beautiful, smart and compassionate. She had been through some very dark days in her young life. Maybe someday she and Sam would reach a level of trust where they would share their experiences. Time would tell.

As Sam pulled into the gate of his home, he realized how different he felt than when he left to make this trip. He could hardly believe it. He was inspired by Allison's personal passion to do her job because of her trauma. Perhaps this was a lesson for him. He needed to do the same.

Clearly, Sam didn't need to practice law to make money. He already had more than he would ever spend. For the first time, Sam began to think outside the box. He wanted to invoke Arthur's wisdom to help him find a way to make a meaningful contribution, to do what he could as an attorney to make some kind of meaningful difference.

When Sam opened the front door, little Max jumped in his arms, full of wet sloppy kisses. Ned smiled at Sam and said they had a great week together. He was happy to be home. There was no place like home. He felt renewed in his spirit, more than he could ever have hoped to feel.

Sam thanked Ned and slipped a few hundred dollars into his hand. Although Ned tried to refuse it, Sam insisted. It was really good to see Ned again. They made plans to have lunch the following week. Sam was ready to get involved with people again, ready to be social. He was happy to be in that space. It was a long time coming. Natalie's death had a greater impact on him than he wanted to acknowledge. It was time to move on.

It was a good week. Sam got back into the swing of things. Max continued to bring Sam his leash. They did their runs together. Sam felt genuinely blessed to have so much joy in his life. It was palpable. He was discovering there was life after Arthur.

Sam and Stephen met at their appointed time. Sam spent more than an hour briefing Stephen on the London conference. He also shared his research on other foundations that were focused on the marriage of helping children and family law. He had put together a skeleton plan of how he thought the Arthur Adams Foundation could be established. Stephen was all ears.

They ended up meeting most of that entire day. They each took sections of the plan and would be responsible for researching and coming up with their best ideas. They finally had a tangible plan. It was coming together. Both of them were encouraged by their progress. They would meet again in one month.

*****

The London conference turned out to be much more than just a meeting across the ocean. It had provided a plausible path for Arthur's foundation. It may have even provided a plausible path for Sam. He was smitten!

Sam felt more excited about meeting Allison than he could ever remember feeling about meeting anyone except for maybe Arthur. She was beautiful, smart, soft and totally pleasant. He had enjoyed spending time with her. He couldn't get enough of her.

Sam had a million things to attend to when he returned from London, not the least of which was meeting with Stephen to consult about the Foundation.

Sam was convinced that combining the law and children's needs was a cause that Arthur would have gotten behind. Stephen concurred. Now, finally, they had a name for the Foundation and had just come up with their mission statement. Now, they had to forge ahead with specific plans to create something very special.

It did not escape Sam's realization that family law was Allison's specialty and he was eager to figure out how she could be incorporated into this project. He didn't even want to admit to himself how much he wanted to find a way to make her a part of his life.

Although Sam's expertise was not in family law, he was a highly esteemed attorney and had the respect of many of his colleagues. This was the glue that brought him and Allison together. Perhaps it would be the key that would lead to something more permanent.

Chapter 9

Allison

In the middle of intensely focused work on the Arthur Adams Foundation, the following week, Sam got a call from Allison. He was delighted to hear from her. After a few minutes of surface conversation, she told him about a new case their firm had just received. She said it would be a difficult one to win and she wondered if she could ask Sam for a consultation. He immediately agreed.

She said it was such an important and urgent case, she wanted to present it to him in person. Her firm was willing to send her to Seattle to meet with him. He agreed to meet with her. They set a time and he agreed to pick her up at the airport.

Sam was filled with anticipation as he contemplated his consultation with Allison. Clearly, the case was very important to her and her firm to send her to Seattle to meet with him. He hoped he could be of help. He also hoped she could be of help to him in helping him formulate plans for the new center.

The week passed quickly. He would be meeting Allison's plane the following morning. He knew this was a professional meeting and he needed to be certain to keep that focus. He was very attracted to her and knew he could not relate to her on that level. This would be challenging.

Sam got to the airport early. He didn't want to risk being late. He was standing at the gate when the passengers were departing. About half way through, he spotted Allison. She had on black slacks and a beautiful red sweater with a matching scarf. She looked lovely.

She spotted him and they moved quickly out of the terminal. She had not checked any luggage. When they got to the car, Sam suggested they meet in Arthur's study. Allison looked surprised but agreed and they were on their way.

Allison was stunned, to put it mildly, as they drove through the iron gate toward the house. When Sam stopped the car, he made it clear to Allison that this was all Arthur's accomplishments, not his. He was simply blessed to be able to live there.

They went directly to the study. On the way, Sam introduced Allison to Max. She picked him up, telling Sam how much she loved dogs. Sam told her Max had been Natalie's dog. She simply looked at him compassionately. No words needed to be spoken.

Over the next several hours, Allison presented a very complex and complicated scenario of the facts of their case. Sam listened intently and took notes. After two hours, Sam began asking his questions.

After six hours, they were discussing whether or not Sam believed this case could be won in front of a jury.

Before he answered, his actual thought was, "What would Arthur say?" Sam took in a deep breath and began asking his questions. Two hours later, they were both exhausted.

Finally, Sam looked at Allison and simply said, "yes." Allison asked, "Yes, what?" Sam said, "Yes, it can be won." Allison was so excited she jumped in his arms and gave him a huge hug. It was all he could do not to respond in kind.

Sam immediately turned the conversation to the nuances of the case. He pointed out very specifically what the jury would need to hear in order to win the case. He didn't think it would be easy, but he did believe it was possible.

Allison took copious notes. She was seriously impressed with Sam's assessment and perceptions of this case. She would never even have thought of the issues he was addressing. She shook her head in amazement. By this time, their heads were swimming and they were both done with thinking about this case.

Sam asked, "How about a glass of wine by the pool?" Allison smiled and said she thought he'd never ask. Sam had some nice snacks to go with it. They poured the wine, gathered the snacks and headed for the pool. They quickly drank the first bottle of wine and were on their second. Allison asked lots of personal questions, although they were not invasive. Sam felt comfortable talking about the answers.

Before they knew it, it was 8 p.m.. Allison asked Sam if she would please drop her off at her hotel. She gathered her briefcase and headed for the car. Little Max was allowed to go with them.

Allison explained she had an early flight back to San Francisco. She thanked Sam profusely. She was so deeply grateful for his amazing legal expertise. He saw the expression of gratitude on her face and believed her.

They agreed to continue their discussion of the case as she and her colleagues prepared for this case. Once again, Sam said he would be as helpful as he possibly could be.

She squeezed his hand as she got out of the car. It had been an immensely productive time for both of them.

As the weeks and months flew by, emails and texts were exchanged nearly everyday between Allison and Sam. Her colleagues had been as equally impressed as Allison regarding Sam's approach to the case. Finally, Allison would be giving the prosecutor's opening statement tomorrow. She had been over it several times with Sam. He had given her confidence that she was, in fact, ready to do this. Time would tell.

Sam could hardly wait to hear from Allison about how the day had gone in court. Finally, she called. He could hear from her tone of voice that she had a good day. He was very happy to hear it. She gave him details from the events of the day. He asked some questions. They spent some time processing it and Sam inquired about the next steps. They were off and running, in more ways than one.

The case lasted four weeks. There had been some very tough cross examinations. Allison called more than once feeling very upset about the events of the day. Sam listened, both on a personal and on a professional level. Sam had a calm demeanor about him that served him well. Allison had come to count on it. Sam had become her confidante. She was beginning to have strong feelings for him but worked hard to keep them to herself.

The case was now in the jury's hands. It was the fourth day of their deliberations. Allison was on pins and needles and was beginning to have serious doubts about winning the case. Finally, the word came down that the jury had reached a decision. Allison was aware of how tense she was feeling as she watched the jury file into the courtroom, all of them looking down.

Finally, the bailiff handed the decision to the judge and he read it. He returned it to the bailiff who gave it to the jury foreman to read. They all stood.

When the verdict was read, tears began to flow freely down Allison's face. The pedophile was convicted and would be serving the rest of his life in prison. Allison knew this would never have happened were it not for Sam. She had no words.

Allison felt far too emotional to talk with Sam in person. She sent him a text: "It's over...we won, thanks to you." Allison began to realize how significant it was that she had approached Sam at the conference in London. What made her do that?

Allison was a strong Christian. Otherwise, she would have been destroyed when she and her sister were kidnapped, raped and beaten when they were only eight years old. Her twin sister had not survived. She almost didn't either. It was a miracle she was found in time. She believed in miracles. She had lived through one. She had always believed and felt that God had His hand on her life. Now she was more sure of it than ever. She really believed Sam had crossed her path for a reason, maybe for several reasons.

Her heart was filled with overwhelming gratitude for him. Yes, it was an important case and she was happy their firm had been successful in prosecuting the case. More to the point, she felt like she was falling in love with Sam.

The next day was Saturday. Her phone rang at 8 a.m. It was Sam. She took a deep breath and answered. He congratulated her and told her he was proud of her. She burst into tears.

Sam didn't say anything for a minute as he realized what was happening. Finally he asked her, "Is everything OK?" When she could catch her breath and speak she said, "Yes, I'm OK.....I guess.....Sam, I need to see you." Sam really didn't know how to respond. He simply said, "OK.... when would you like to make that happen?" Allison said, "The sooner, the better." They talked for a few minutes and decided Sam would fly down in the morning and spend the day with her.

When they hung up, Allison realized how embarrassed she felt. What must Sam be thinking of her

right now? Somehow she was feeling very childlike.…..
vulnerable, a little helpless. She needed to tell Sam how
she was feeling, more about who she was. She felt she
needed to tell him the facts about the trauma in her
life. That would be as difficult as being honest about her
feelings for him. This felt like a do or die moment.

She laid awake most of the night trying to formulate
what she was going to say and how she needed to say it.
For being an attorney, somehow she felt like a blithering
idiot. She had absolutely no idea how she was going to
tell him her feelings. Before she knew it, it was time to
leave for the airport. Sam was on his way right now.

Allison was at the gate when Sam arrived. It was a
sunny day. Allison was thinking it might be a good idea
to visit a park. They could take a nice walk around the
lake. She knew just the place. He greeted her warmly.
They embraced in a gentle hug and headed to her car.
The park was a short distance away.

Allison thanked Sam for making the trip. She told
him how she felt when she hung up from their phone
conversation. Sam assured her that she didn't have any
reason to be embarrassed.

When they got to the park and started to walk
around the lake, Allison asked Sam to simply listen to all
that she had to say before he spoke. He agreed.

She started by telling him the ugly and traumatic
story of her kidnapping. She left out most of the details
but made it a point to tell him how it had affected her
emotionally. Sam listened intently.

She had spent a decade in therapy in an effort to deal with watching her sister be murdered, surviving rape and torture for a week. She really felt death would have been easier. She went on to explain she believed she survived because of her personal faith in God. Her faith had always been the source of hope in her life. She believed God helped her survive this ordeal in order to grow up, graduate law school and put away pedophiles as she had done this week, thanks to Sam. There is no way he could know how much his help meant to her.

The next part was harder to share. She realized that when the verdict was read in the courtroom and the tears ran down her face that she loved Sam. She was even thinking maybe she was falling in love with Sam, something she never dreamed possible.

She felt she needed to tell him. She stopped and looked deep into his eyes. He simply reached out and held her close. No words were spoken. She started to cry.

Sam said, "OK, It's my turn now....The first time I met you in London, I was unbelievably attracted to you. I was so afraid it showed. When you came to my house, I had those same feelings all over again. I have been working overtime to keep our relationship professional but I've wanted to make it personal from the first time I met you. I'm so sorry for your painful childhood. Sometime I will tell you about my painful childhood.…...Actually, Allison, I think that I am falling in love with you also...." He kissed her.

They continued their walk around the lake, holding hands. The sun was shining. It was a beautiful day. Their hearts were smiling.

They decided to go to Allison's house and have some lunch. They ate some cold chicken and opened a bottle of wine. Sam shared the story of his childhood with Allison. He watched as the tears rolled down her face as he talked. She could hardly believe that Sam had suffered about as much as she had. They just held each other. They were both feeling incredibly loving and loved. Neither of them had ever experienced these feelings before. They didn't even know they were possible.

Sam had an early flight back to Seattle the following morning. They got very little sleep that night. They talked for hours. They were trying to stay focused and make plans to spend as much time together as they could. They wanted to see where this relationship would take them. Right now, they both wanted to spend the rest of their lives together.

When Sam arrived back home, the whole world looked different to him now. He really felt he had found the love of his life and was intent on figuring out how they could join their lives together. It would be a process he and Allison would figure out together.

Over the next several months, Sam and Allison were inseparable. They flew back and forth frequently and their plans seemed to unfold naturally. Sam had proposed and Allison accepted. Now it was a matter of figuring out the details.

Allison had her heart set on being married in her church. Sam was fine with that. It would be a very small wedding with only a few close friends. Neither of them had family. Allison would quit her job and move to Seattle to live with Sam. They were both so excited. They felt very blessed and very loved. If they decided they wanted to accept some legal cases, they could work them together. This felt totally compatible. Arthur would have approved heartily. There was no doubt about that.

The wedding was in one week. Even with it being very small, there were a lot of details to take care of. Allison wanted to find the perfect dress, her favorite flowers and a catered small dinner for the wedding party. It would be a beautiful simple event.

The wedding was perfect. Sam and Allison looked like the perfect couple, both outside and inside. Their love for one another was so apparent to everyone. People seemed to enjoy themselves. There was nothing pretentious about any part of it. It was simply a beautiful Christian wedding.

Sam and Allison decided they would live in Seattle and spend time settling in before they decided where they wanted to go for their honeymoon. They didn't feel any pressure at all. They could go whenever they decided it was the right time.

Everything had fallen into place beautifully. They married and were living in Seattle. This was an adjustment for Allison but she was so happy to be with Sam, it wasn't difficult. This was a dream come true for both of them.

The next year was spent making the house their own. They added some new furniture, changed some window treatments, updated the kitchen and changed some of the carpeting in the master bedroom and the study. Now it was really beginning to feel like their own.

They had established some routine. Max learned he could bring his leash to either Sam or Allison and their walk would happen. Everyone was happy. All was well.

Word had gotten around that Sam had gotten married and that his law practice was not a priority during this time.

About the time they were starting to think about their honeymoon, he started receiving requests for representation in court.

This motivated Sam and Allison to plan and execute their honeymoon plans. They were considering Hawaii, Fiji Islands or a British Isles tour, especially since they had met in London. Finally, they decided on Hawaii. It was simply beautiful. They were headed to Maui for two weeks.

Those two weeks were a blur. They went by so fast, they could hardly believe it was time to return to Seattle. They spent a lot of time by the ocean. They snorkeled, they swam, they had so many lunches and dinners by the ocean. They had lots of pictures of incredible sunsets. It had been a very spectacular time. They had spent hours talking and talking. There was so much to say. They never seemed to run out of things to share with each other.

Flying back home, their thoughts turned to their work. What were their wishes about their practices? They would have to wait and see what was available. They were certain it would all fall together. Allison was hoping there would be at least one that involved helping children. Time would tell.

Allison loved Sam's church. She had met many of the people Sam knew, mostly from his time with Arthur; also, his brief time with Natalie. They fit right in as a couple and were beginning to have lots of social times with other couples. They loved their new found friends and saw them weekly as they attended Sunday services.

Allison had requested of Sam that they prayed together each evening before going to sleep, just a brief prayer. Sam agreed. It was a nice way to end the day and fall asleep peacefully. They were both filled with deep gratitude they had found each other and become life partners. It was more than either of them ever dreamed possible.

The following year was spent in solidifying the marriage, really getting to know one another inside and out, understanding each other's views as attorneys and how they wanted to invest their energies. So far, they seemed to have been on the same page with most everything. Life was good.

Allison agreed with Sam that establishing a foundation linking children's needs and family law was an outstanding idea. She and Sam and Stephen met and began ironing out their business plan. It was complex and very complicated. It was an exciting project for all of them.

Sam was finishing up a case which would be concluding soon and would then have more time to devote to this project.

Sam, Allison and Stephen each agreed to clear their calendars completely for the next month.

They would start at 7 a.m. and spend as much of each day as they needed. They would begin to actually hammer out all of the details of making this a profoundly important foundation for helping children. They wanted it to be a world-renowned prototype which would be the first of many foundations. Clearly, they had their work cut out for them.

It would all have to begin with a massive remodelling project. The entire mansion would require a face lift. They needed to hire consultants to help them manage the best plan.

For the next year, Sam and Allison devoted most of their time and attention to all of the legalities into making Arthur's home a place to heal children. For now, Sam, Stephen and Allison would serve as the CEOs, in charge of running the home. Sam wondered if Ned would have any interest in being the CFO since he was a CPA. Sam would advertise many of the positions in the New York Times, the Washington Post, USA Today, and many other sources. They would post their positions and allow six months to interview suitable candidates. They had a projected opening date on June 1 of the following year. That should give them plenty of time.

They could take 10 or 11 children at a time. They would each have their own bedroom. Each was assigned to an in-house guardian. Each would have a daily schedule specifically to address their personal issues. It would likely be different for each child.

Staff would include a psychiatrist, 2 psychologists, one physician on retainer, one nurse, one chaplain, 2 social workers, an equine expert, a marketing specialist, a nutritionist, an exercise physiologist, a lifeguard, an office manager, 4 cooks, 6 housekeepers and 3 assistant housekeepers, a chauffeur, and two corporate attorneys. This was a dream in the making. There were likely thousands of children who could benefit from coming here to heal.

After six months of exhausting resumes and conducting interviews, it was becoming a reality the doors would soon be opening. Requests for admission were pouring in. Each one of them would need to be carefully examined for appropriateness at this facility. This would require much training and many man hours. Clearly, Sam and Allison had bitten off an enormous chunk of work.

Six horses had been purchased, all appropriate for children. An equine expert was in charge of designing the stables, hiring appropriate staff and designating safe paths for the children to ride.

A children's pool had been installed near the adult pool. Lifeguards would be hired to ensure the children's safety.

There were a million details demanding their attention. Sam and Allison were weary from all of the work. They had redecorated the entire household. Everything was brought up to date. All bathrooms were inspected and changes were made. It was beautiful.

An open house was scheduled one week before opening day. A general invitation had gone out to many hundreds of people. Some were coming all the way from the East Coast. They were ready.

*****

Clearly it was not only Sam who was smitten. He and Allison had come together and committed their love and their future life together. Neither of them could have possibly understood what this would require of each of them.

The pieces all appeared to be fitting together beautifully. Not only their love but also their professions were intertwined. They were now part of realizing Arthur's dream. It was all such a privilege.

It was an enormous undertaking they had just put in place. There would be many issues they would face and need to work out as they progressed. This Foundation had received world-wide attention and was on the radar around the world. It needed to function like a well-oiled machine.

This event was actually a very big miracle. Both Sam and Allison had survived horrific traumas in their young lives. They were both lucky to be alive. The ways in which Arthur and Sam met and the way in which Sam and Allison met were all unlikely scenarios. Yet, this is the reality of the way in which life, and a crooked path, works.

Keeping a positive attitude and focus can take all of us places we never dreamed. Sometimes the dreams really do become reality.

Sometimes, our dreams have a very high price tag attached to them. Sometimes they create a very crooked path.

CHAPTER 10

The Foundation

The house was perfect. It could not have looked better. A year's worth of work never looked better. There would, of course, be a learning curve and changes would, no doubt, need to be made. They were up to it!

A lavish champagne brunch was served that Saturday morning with specific guests invited. It would be open to the public beginning at 1 p.m. They had received over 300 RSVPs. This would be a busy day, no doubt.

The champagne brunch was mostly for the new employees and their families. They were made especially welcome. There was a calm and pleasant feeling that day as everyone mingled, getting to know one another. There was a positive spirit in the air. Sam was certain Arthur was there, feeling very pleased. Sam had made certain that their board of directors included Arthur's closest attorney friends.

At 1 p.m. the gates opened and it was non-stop until 8 p.m. that evening. By the time everyone had gone home, Sam and Allison climbed into the shower, fell into bed and slept until 10AM the next morning. They missed church.

As they sipped their morning coffee by the pool, both Sam and Allison expressed how positively they believed the opening had gone. Some excellent suggestions were made that needed to be pursued. There was a basket where everyone was invited to leave their card. Sam and Allison would enjoy going through them to understand who had been there. They were not able to interact with every guest. They felt they had a treasure trove of potential resources for whatever they might need. Right now, they needed rest.

So far, five children had been accepted as clients and would be arriving in a week. Three girls and two boys were arriving from five different parts of the country. Each had a very personal story. Clearly, they had their work cut out for them. This week would include long staff meetings. Every detail would be made clear, in writing. Everyone had a duty to perform and each would be held to a high standard.

Each child was assigned an "unseen angel," a friend who would help each child, whatever their needs might be. This week's meeting was designed to assess each child's needs and prepare their daily schedule. It would be different for each child. This process was very time consuming. Everyone's input was respectfully heard and considered.

There had been ten applications which were not accepted, for various reasons. These included children who saw dead people, sexual predators, autism, uncontrolled rage issues, pyromania, multiple personalities, animal abuse or those who were suicidal. They were deemed as being more appropriate for facilities specifically designed to treat their issues.

Soon they would be welcoming their first little people. Tracey, Amy and Emily had each come from broken homes. They each had a dark history of neglect and abuse. They had experienced parental violence toward them. They were poorly adjusted, extremely fearful children between the ages of five and ten. Jimmy and Jerry had been severely physically and sexually abused. They were both five years old.

Allison suggested that the staff meet every morning at 7:55a.m. for a joint brief prayer before they started their day. The chaplain would lead. They all agreed.

Besides the specific expertise of each of the staff, they were carefully screened for their levels of compassion. It was as important to Sam and Allison as expertness in their field. They believed they had assembled a very caring group of people to help these children. Love was the answer.

Emily was the first child to arrive. She was seven years old. She was from New Mexico. She had been severely abused by her mother's boyfriend. She appeared shy and very thin. She clung to a small teddy bear. She nodded her head when asked a question but did not speak. She was taken to a lovely room designed specifically for a little girl. She just stood in the room, holding her bear tight and asked, "Is this for me?"

Next came Amy. She was 8 years old, from Kentucky. She had been beaten and starved, removed from her home by social services. She was crying and covered her face when asked a question. She was lovingly taken to her room.

Tracey was ten years old, from Texas. She was found living on the streets of Dallas. She was a runaway. In time, she would disclose her story. She appeared angry and asked, "So, where do I sleep?"

Jimmy was a sweet little blonde boy who looked lost. He stared at everyone. He walked around the house and looked at everything. He was taken by the hand to his new room.

Jerry was the last to arrive. He was also five years old, from Oregon. Jerry seemed happy to be there. He said how much he liked "the big house." He seemed fascinated that he would have a room all to himself.

For the first time, the children were in the house and were now their responsibility. Each of the assigned 'angels' were with each of the children, answering their questions and showing them around their new home.

The contract for each child was for a month at a time. Each child would be thoroughly evaluated after each 30 day period. There would be a careful assessment of their progress, or lack thereof. The staff would decide the best course of treatment as each child's progress unfolded. It would be a challenging process to manage.

The first day, bedtime seemed to be the most challenging time for the children, as well as for the staff. The children remembered bad things happening to them at night. The children were given a snack of their choosing. Their night light was always kept on. They were each given a whistle which they were to use if they woke in the night and needed someone to help them. These additional steps at bedtime seemed to help them feel more at ease, especially the younger children. The first night was quiet. No whistles were to be heard.

The staff were getting to know each of the children. They were very different from one another and it soon became apparent just how different they really were. Emily did not like to be touched and she hated milk. Jimmy and Jerry had rooms next to one another. Jimmy was found at the bottom of Jerry's bed, sound asleep, the first morning. He was afraid to be alone. Tracey was the first to the breakfast table and demanded bacon and eggs, toast and coffee. Amy said she just wanted some juice, no food.

They were up and running. Each child's daily activities were different. They always had their special angel with them for support. The children always took their meals together. This enabled them to get to know one another.

One of the biggest issues for all of the children was trust. No one had enough of it. The staff needed to be gentle, kind and demonstrate caring, helpfulness and patience. These were very damaged little people.

They quickly got into their routines. By the second week, it was clear which children liked what and whom. The daily staff meetings were interesting as staff shared their perceptions. All of the children appeared to love the horses, except for Jimmy. They scared him. They all loved the swimming pool, except for Amy. She was afraid of the water. Amy wasn't eating much and staff were concerned about her weight. The nutritionist was looking for ways to increase her caloric intake. They did not want to see her turn into a full blown anorexic or bulimia victim. She was a sweet little girl but her wounds were toxic and dark. She would need extra help.

Tracey's anger and demanding personality was challenging to the staff. They experienced her as angry and often disrespectful. Turning this around would take time and great patience. Staff were encouraged not to get hooked by her anger. She wanted people to treat her badly so she could feel justified in not getting close to anyone.

After one month, each of the children were evaluated. All would continue in the program.

The second month, two more children were added. They were sibling orphans whose parents had perished in a plane crash. They had enormous adjustment issues. They never left each other's sight. They stuck together like glue. They were 6 and 8 years old, brother and sister. They shared a room.

The following month, two more children were added. They were brothers from Guatemala. Their migrant parents had not survived the journey to the US border. They were orphans who needed to learn survival skills. They were four and five years old.

Finally, the last of the ten children arrived. Her name was Tiffany. She was seven years old and had an unusual history. She had witnessed the murder of her parents and suffered from post traumatic stress disorder. Clearly, the staff had their work cut out for them.

Sam and Allison were the powerful leaders of this organization. They purposely stayed in the background as much as possible. They were attorneys who knew how to delegate to people with skills they didn't possess. They were on the scene each day, observing all of the children. They were nonchalantly part of the landscape. The children had no idea who they were. That worked for Sam and Allison.

The foundation was now up and running. They were delighted with how well it seemed to be working. Progress was being documented and praised endlessly. Each of the children were noticeably different from when they arrived. At some point, it would be very hard to let them go.

Sam, Stephen and Allison had a final meeting. The Foundation was up and running. They had done their jobs. Now it would be a matter of managing the day to day issues that would soon be apparent. All of the players were in place to deal with whatever was needed. They could step back now and continue with their other legal responsibilities. They toasted with a glass of champagne and a smile.

*****

Reality had now set in.

Treating traumatized children was one of the most difficult challenges in the world. The beauty here was that both Allison and Sam understood the reality of the challenge because they had experienced them.

This Foundation didn't just spring up overnight because someone thought it would be a kind thing to try to help needy children. It had its roots in overcoming trauma. It had its roots in grounding children in unconditional love.

This Foundation was the only one of its kind in all the world. It was a multi-billion dollar corporation designed for one purpose: healing.

Some would say they created a miracle. Others might say they had created a monster.

Time would tell

CHAPTER 11

The Courtroom

O ne day, Sam received a call from the pastor of their church. He inquired of Sam if he would be willing to meet with one of the couples in the church with a dire issue with legal implications. He said it involved a child. Sam agreed to meet with them the following week.

The couple was one he hardly knew. He was a physician and she was a nurse. They had three children. One of the children had become a concern to them. She was eleven years old, in 6th grade. Her personality had changed. She was fearful, angry and didn't want to go to school. Try as they might, the parents could not get her to tell them what the problem was. Eventually, they sought professional help from a child psychiatrist.

Through a process, mostly of drawing pictures, it was believed that Shelly was being sexually assaulted by her male teacher. The psychiatrist knew it was her word against his until they had her physically examined. There was evidence of vaginal penetration and tearing. Eventually, Shelly told her parents what happened to her and why she didn't want to go to school anymore.

The parent's anger was palpable. They were at the point of needing to file some kind of legal charges against him. That is why they wanted to consult with Sam before making their decision.

For the next two hours, Sam took careful notes to be certain he had all of the facts. He said he would need to spend some hours going over them and formulating what a case against this man might entail. He also wanted his wife's input since this was her specialty as an attorney. They agreed to meet the following Monday, all four of them.

Sam returned home and went through his notes with Allison. She had some very relevant questions Sam hadn't asked. It was good she would be joining them for the Monday meeting. In spite of this little girl's pain, this was exactly the kind of case Allison lived for, to prosecute pedophiles. It pleased her to be part of this process.

On Monday, the four of them met. Sam went through the timeline of events and traced the assaults. Allison asked to see the medical reports on Allison's injuries and evidence of penetration. Finally, they requested to have Shelly present at their next meeting. After all of that had taken place, Sam believed they would be certain of how to charge this man.

Sam and Allison continued to discuss all angles of the case for hours in Arthur's study. They came up with more relevant questions that needed to be answered. Finally, they would meet Shelly and assess what kind of witness they believed she would be. Her testimony could be videotaped for the jury so as to not inflict any more pain on her. All of this would need to be considered as the case unfolded.

After one more meeting with Shelly present, they were ready to proceed. A sheriff's deputy arrived at the school, charged the teacher and took him away in handcuffs.

The teacher pleaded "not guilty." He was actually a very popular teacher who was well liked. When word got out that he was being charged for sexual assault, and by whom, there was a lot of backlash against Shelly. Her little life seemed to be going from bad to worse. Her parents removed her from the school and put her in a private school in the next town. Allison was especially sensitive to Shelly's pain because of her own childhood history.

A trial date was set. Sam and Allison would serve as the prosecuting attorneys. They believed they had a solid case and were ready to pursue it.

The trial lasted three weeks. It was very painful for Shelly and her family. Facts and nuances about the case were presented for all to see and hear. The effects of all of this on Shelly's young life would likely mean years of personal therapy.

Child trauma is violent and terrifying, not easily overcome. At one point, she broke down on the stand during cross examination from a defense attorney. He suggested that she wanted to be her teacher's favorite student and did lots of things to invite his attention.

He could not have been more wrong but Shelly was traumatized by hearing that remark. She couldn't go on. The judge dismissed her.

The jury had the case for three days. Word had just come that they had reached a verdict. The jurors filed back into the courtroom and the verdict was read by the judge, then read aloud by the jury foreman. He was found guilty. Sentencing would occur in one month. In the meantime, he was to be held without bail.

Even though Shelly came from a wealthy family and they could afford to pay legal fees, Sam and Allison gave their time pro bono. It was their gift to Shelly and her family. They were just pleased they could help them find justice. They were also pleased this man would never be able to hurt any other children.

That night, Allison cooked Sam's favorite meal and they enjoyed it by candlelight around the pool. They were so pleased at the outcome of the trial. They both felt they had used their legal talents for good. It felt good. Sam was sure Arthur was smiling at them.

Sam and Allison were somewhat still in their honeymoon phase. They had just tackled a case together and had a positive outcome. They were able to create a very positive outcome and make a difference for good. Their love and their skills were paving the way for them to create their dreams and realize them.

This likely cannot last forever. Just up ahead may be a very sharp turn in their crooked path.

CHAPTER 12

The Senator

One day Sam received a call from a colleague of Arthur's. He identified himself as being one of Arthur's greatest cheerleaders. He knew he had mentored Sam. He wanted to inquire if Sam was open to accepting a new case. As it turned out, this was a senator from another state. He had a colleague, also a senator, whose son had been kidnapped. They had just found his body that morning. He was five years old. The perpetrator had been arrested. They were looking for a prosecutor for the case. Would Sam be interested?

The foundation was now up and running smoothly, Sam considered this might be a case to consider, especially when the request came from a friend of Arthur's. Sam asked him to send him all of the information he had about the case and he would get back to him before the end of the week. They agreed. Sam was very clear that he was mostly a defense attorney but had some degree of comfort and confidence as a prosecutor.

Sam told Allison about the call and asked her what she thought. She agreed with Sam that he needed to carefully assess the facts of the case before making a decision. What came to light when they received the file was that the alleged perpetrator of the crime was a US senator. This gave him pause. It was alleged that he hired the gunman to kidnap and kill the child as part of a personal vendetta. The senator fervently denied it. This would be a very high profile case. Did Sam really want to accept this case?

Against his better judgment, Sam accepted the case primarily because of Allison's encouragement. She was sensitive to the loss of the young boy. Such a heinous act needed to be prosecuted by someone who knew how to win. Sam immediately requested co-counsel. He selected Allison. They would jointly take on this case.

As they began to research this crime it became obvious how complex and complicated it was. The senator accused of the crime believed he had been betrayed by the boy's father. His motive was vengeance. The child had been beaten to death with a hammer.

As the pretrial motions were filed and preliminary papers were drawn, the pressure of this case became darker and heavier. The child's mother had to be hospitalized because of her son's horrendous death. No one was faring well in this hideous case.

Finally, it was time for opening statements. Allison gave the initial summary of the case. It was stellar. She had a strength and poise which attracted the jury. She spoke with obvious passion about the death of the child and the way he died. There were tears in the eyes of some of the jurors. She had hit an opening home run. From there, Sam took over and continued presenting the prosecution's case. This took two days.

The senator had hired a nationally recognized high-level attorney. Sam knew him from other trials. He also knew that Arthur didn't think much of him. He was, however, prolific in the courtroom. Sam knew he had his work cut out for him.

The perpetrator took the stand and spelled out how he came to be involved in this case. He gave details of what he wanted done and how he wanted it done. He was paid $100,000.00. On cross examination it was clear that many of the details of his account could not be evidenced. It was his word against the senator's.

After several days of witnesses, the accused senator took the stand. It was time for Sam to cross examine him. This was going to be the bottom line of the case. Everyone knew it. Sam thundered away at him. He asked him everything from his relationship with his colleague to how he regarded children. He was neither married nor had children. He was known to have a bad temper and to be vindictive.

At one point, it was clear the senator was getting very angry and defensive. His attorney called for a recess. The judge allowed it. Court was done for today. As it continued tomorrow., Sam would have another shot at him. He had a lot to think about that night. This was the very last witness in the trial before final arguments and then it would go to the jury. Now was the time to strike while the iron was hot.

Allison was not with him in the courtroom that day. She was not feeling well and had stayed home. He called her when the court adjourned but got her voicemail. He said he hoped she was feeling better and that he was on his way home.

When Sam arrived home, he was immediately aware that something was very wrong. Allison's purse and cell phone were in the house but she wasn't. There was no sign of her. Sam was terrified. His first thought was that the senator had her taken in order to ensure his acquittal in the courtroom.

Knowing the trauma she had endured in her early life, Sam couldn't even imagine how retraumatized she must be feeling right now. He was beside himself. He knew the police wouldn't do anything until she had been missing for 72 hours. By that time, the trial would be over and the senator would likely go free.

At 10 p.m. that night, Sam's phone rang. It was Allison. She told him she had been taken, that she was safe but that he needed to do what they told him or she would never see him again. She was sobbing. At that point, a male voice came on the line and told him if he ever wanted to see his wife again, he better see to it that the senator was not convicted. He hung up.

What was he to do? It was time for court to begin. He had been up all night. The judge called the court to order. The senator retook his oath and was back on the stand. He was up to bat. Sam took a deep breath and indicated he had no further questions. The senator smiled. At that point, the judge told the senator he could step down and began giving the jury instructions.

Sam quickly left the courtroom before anyone had a chance to ask him anything. He drove straight home, got in the shower for a very long time and fell onto his bed. When would this be over?

The jury deliberated for two days. The word was the jury had reached a verdict and were headed back into the courtroom. Sam could hardly get his breath. Time seemed endless before he finally heard the verdict for the senator, "Guilty." Sam's heart sank.

Even though he had backed off at the point he was asked, it hadn't really made any difference. They still found him guilty. Sam left the courtroom and drove directly to the police station. He poured out his entire story and simply sank into a chair. What if he never saw her again?

A week after the trial, he still had not heard from Allison. It was the greatest grief he had ever known. Nothing mattered to him as much as she did. Part of him wanted to slit the throat of the senator. He knew he had to let the police handle it.

The police were following every lead. There were hundreds of them, but to no avail. It had now been three months since Allison had disappeared. There had been no word of any kind. He wasn't sure he was capable of knowing how to make it through the next five minutes without her. This was an unbelievable nightmare. His life felt "over."

After a year, Allison was declared legally dead. Sam had dealt with the agonizing pain for more than a year now. The effect it had on him was to advertise to the world that he was open for business to prosecute any and all of the world's worst felons. He would use his legal skills to do as much good and bring as much pain to perpetrators as possible. He was on a mission. His life would never be the same

Sam turned the running of the foundation over to a competent attorney. He would always be grateful for what he and Allison had envisioned and built together. However, his life circumstances had changed now and he was on a different path, his crooked path. He hated it. It seemed his whole life had been about death and pain. Sam was now full of rage.

Sam accepted and won every single case he accepted for the next 5 years. His rage drove him in ways he had never experienced before. He envisioned every perpetrator as the one who took his beloved Allison from him. His rage was the source of his energy. He had become a very different person. He hardly recognized himself. He wasn't certain he even knew who he had become. He didn't know whether or not he even had any interest in knowing that person. As far as he was concerned, his life was over.

Sam was about to have his 50th birthday. Big whoop. Who cared anyway? Not him. Sam felt at the very end of himself. He was a destitute multi-millionaire who had never felt more lost. He was looking up to see the bottom.

One morning his phone rang. A woman's voice asked if he was Sam. He acknowledged that it was. She said,

"I might know something about the disappearance of your wife." Sam didn't say anything. Was this some kind of sick scam? Why would anyone bother to make this call at this point? She had been gone for almost 6 years. He confronted the caller. She said she understood why he didn't trust what she was saying but that she really did know. Sam just listened. "What do you know?" "She was sold into trafficking. She was shipped out of the country. Last I heard, she was still alive." "Why are you just telling me this now?" The woman said, "I've read how much good you have done in starting a special place to help children and you put away bad guys......I recently escaped."

Sam said impatiently, "Tell me what I need to know."

The woman said, "They shipped her off to Qatar along with me and two other women. They kept us on a yacht. She is the sheik's favorite in his harem." Sam thought he was going to vomit. "How do I know any of this is true? Do you have any evidence?"

The woman said, "I was part of that same harem. I escaped." She said she had gotten to know Allison while she was there. "They keep her drugged and high, 24/7. One day she told me about you, how much she loved you and longed to be back with you."

By this time, Sam was hooked. It was the only lead he'd had in nearly 6 years. He asked her for the name of the ship. She told him. She said he would never hear from her again. It was too dangerous but she would say a prayer that he might find her and bring her home."

Sam had no idea if he was talking to a total whack job or whether this woman was telling the truth. Either way, he felt compelled to check it out. The first thing he did was pick up the phone to call the best private investigator he knew. He admonished him to meet him in one hour. Sam was there within 20 minutes.

Sam was talking fast as he explained what had just happened. Actually, he was hyperventilating. The private investigator asked him to slow down and give him some facts. Sam told him the name of a ship in Qatar owned by a sheik. He wanted it checked out immediately, no matter what the cost. He was told his wife was being held captive there and had been for the past 6 years. He asked him when he could leave and go there?

Greg raised his eyebrows, took a deep breath and asked Sam if he was really thinking rationally. Sam locked eyes with him and said, "It's the only sane moment I've had in 6 years. GO!"

The next week was the longest week of Sam's life. He was in touch with Greg six or eight times per day. During that time, Greg had done some exhaustive detective work and discovered a link between the prosecuted senator and ties to the middle east, specifically Qatar.

Greg had finally reached Qatar that morning and was busy finding the ship. Every minute was agonizing for Sam. He didn't know about the laws in Qatar, whether or not they could show just legal cause why Allison should be returned to the USA. Right now, he didn't even know if she was there. It was the greatest hope he had in years.

Sam had never prayed harder in his whole life for God to answer his prayer and bring Allison back to him. He waited for his phone to ring. Finally it did. Greg had located the ship. He was contemplating going to the police station and inquiring about getting aboard.. Sam had tried researching the law in Qatar, but was very unclear about the laws there. He had never been to that part of the world and knew nothing about it.

Greg located the ship and inquired of the authorities how he might get aboard. He relayed to them the reporting of an American citizen being held there against her will. He bribed them with $1,000.00 American money in cash if they could make it happen. He had with him a picture of Allison, at least the way she used to look. He gave it to them to authenticate his story. After they conferred for a few minutes in a language he didn't understand, they took his money and agreed to get him on board. It was clear to him that without the bribe money, it wouldn't be happening.

As they boarded the ship, the man in charge told Greg that the sheik was not there today. He was out of the country. He took this as a good sign. Finally, they were actually on board the ship. The officer told the man in charge they wanted to spend a few minutes looking around.

They went below deck and started knocking on doors, looking for Allison. They had no idea if she was even there what she might look like now. The officer spoke their language and asked them about the sheik's women. A few of them identified themselves. He asked if there were any others. They looked at each other. One of them nodded and said there was one more. She was kept upstairs next to the sheik's personal bedroom.

They went upstairs and were directed to his quarters. They were very lavish. There was one room next to his. Greg knocked softly on the door. There was no answer. He knocked again and heard a kind of soft moaning coming from inside. The door was locked. The officer directed for the door to be opened. Inside they found her, handcuffed to the bed, nude and glassy-eyed. Clearly she was drugged.

The officer used his own key to remove the handcuffs. She saw them and pulled the sheet over her body. She had coal black very long hair. Greg asked her, "Are you Allison?" She stared at him and said nothing. She took a deep breath and barely whispered, "Yes….I am Allison."

Greg looked at the officer and asked if he could take her off of the ship. The officer questioned her and asked if she was a US citizen. She shook her head yes. He asked if she had been brought there against her will. Again, she nodded yes. This was enough for the officer to release her into Greg's custody. They dressed her and quickly left the ship.

Headed for the marina now, Greg told Allison that he had been sent there by Sam to take her home. She burst into tears. It took a few days to process Allison's information since she had no identification. Also, it took some time to get the drugs out of her system. Finally, they boarded the first flight headed for Seattle. She felt absolutely numb. She did not talk at all during the flights. It was clear how fragile she was. This was not going to be an easy transition.

When Sam got word Allison had been found and was coming home, he dropped to his knees, covered his face and cried like a baby. He was totally overcome with emotion. Over and over he kept saying, "Thank you God, Thank you God, Thank you God....." He meant it from the depths of his soul.

He would always be so grateful for the unseen angel who contacted him and told him where she was. He couldn't even imagine the shape Allison must be in or what she had to endure. Whatever it was, he believed he had enough love to help her heal.

The plane was arriving near midnight. Sam had been at the terminal for more than an hour. He couldn't begin to describe all that he was feeling. No matter what her condition, he had to remember she was the love of his life. No matter what.

They had to take four flights to get back to Seattle. He couldn't begin to imagine their level of fatigue. He would be giving Greg an enormous tip for what he was able to accomplish. He felt he owed him his life. He was so grateful for the blessing of all of Arthur's friends. There were no words.

The plane landed. Passengers were deplaning. His eyes were fixed on every passenger as they came through the door. Finally he saw Greg. He knew Allison had to be next. He had never seen her with long black hair before.

It took him a minute to recognize her. He walked straight up to her and opened his arms. She fell into them with deep sobs. She was inconsolable. He thanked Greg who understood he needed to vanish and leave them alone. Allison had no luggage. He nearly had to carry her to the car. No words were spoken.

As they drove home, her head was resting on his shoulder. She hadn't spoken and didn't speak all the way to the house. When they arrived, she turned to him and touched his face. She buried her head into his chest, sobbed convulsively and said nothing. Several minutes passed.

Once inside the house, Sam poured them each a glass of wine. He was hoping this would help to relax Allison. He was not asking her any questions, not forcing her to speak. He knew that would happen when she was ready.

She was still as beautiful as ever. How he did love her and hoped he could convey the depth of his love to her. He tried to speak but was overcome with emotion. Finally, he just reached out and held her. They cried together for nearly an hour. There were no words.

Now that he had Allison back safely, he was ready to go after whomever had taken her and committed this heinous deed. He was committed to seeing them rot in a prison cell. He knew he needed to wait until Allison was ready to speak. That probably wouldn't be anytime soon.

Several days passed. Allison slept an unbelievable amount of time. She had eaten very little and didn't want Sam to leave the house. She wanted him to hold her. She just needed to be held indefinitely. Sam was beginning to feel challenged with his patience. He really wanted her to talk with him.

He took her into the shower with him. They took a very long shower together. He washed her hair and bathed her. He toweled her off, put her in her robe and sat her down at the kitchen table. He asked, "Allison, what do you remember, honey?"

She stared at him with vacant eyes. Finally she said, "They took me. They hurt me. They tortured me." She started to cry. Sam simply held her. That was probably enough questions for today. Sam knew it would be very challenging when she returned but this was more than he had envisioned. She was very very damaged. He needed to get her to a physician and have her thoroughly checked out. He didn't want to retraumatize her in the process. She seemed terrified of everything.

Finally, it struck him. He would place Max in her arms and see what kind of response that would evoke in her. Little Max looked up at Allison and started licking her face. Allison smiled and began petting him. Then she held him tight. She remembered him. She said his name, "Max, little Max..." This was a hopeful sign for Sam. He made it a point to keep Max around as much as possible. He slept on their bed right beside Allison. She would reach out and touch him. He was a comforting presence for her.

After the physician had seen Allison, he told Sam that she was experiencing severe post traumatic stress syndrome that would last a very long time. She was having constant flashbacks which retraumatized her over and over. She had likely been through more trauma and torture than either of them could imagine. He predicted it would take her a very long time to come out of this. He also theorized that the massive amount of drugs she had been given had impacted her nervous system. She had a lot of physical and psychological challenges to overcome. Sam would need to be incredibly patient. He prescribed her antidepressant medication and gave them a referral to a psychiatrist.

One day Sam asked her who took her. She looked at him and said, "Ned took me. He told me you were hurt and I needed to go to you." Sam was dumbfounded. Ned???? Was she really certain this was the person? Again she repeated, "Yes….Ned."

Sam dialed Ned's number and told him he was in the car on his way over to his house. He needed to speak to him. Sam told Ned that Allison had identified him as the one who had taken her on that fateful day.

Ned broke down in tears.."They made me do it. The senator had strong ties with a Middle Eastern sheik in Qatar who was involved with sex trafficing. They said if I didn't they would kill my wife, or worse. I'm so sorry Sam. You have no idea how much pain and guilt I have suffered. I am SO sorry."

Sam replied, "You son of a bitch….you thought I would never find out. I can't believe you call yourself a Christian. By the way, You're fired!" He slammed the door and walked out.

Sam was ready to file legal proceedings against Ned. He would file them the first chance he got. How sad to be so wrong about someone you thought was your friend. He was dumbfounded and beyond angry. Feeling betrayed was one of the worst feelings in the world.

In spite of all the pain, they were making progress. Sam reported Ned to the police detectives who had been handling Allison's kidnapping. They went to his house and arrested him. They took him downtown and took his statement and the details of his actions. The dots were beginning to be connected. It was all starting to come together.

Little Max seemed to be the most comforting to Allison. She bonded with him in a powerful way. She seemed to feel safe when he was around. She was beginning to come back, or so it felt. She was talking more now and had explained how she had ended up in Qatar. It was not a pretty story. Her years as a sex slave with the sheik was what kept her alive. What a torturous life it was. He used her in unmerciful ways. Everyday, Sam saw signs of progress in her. It was very slow but she was coming back. He asked God to please give her strength and give him patience.

Sam asked Allison if she would like to go to the hairdressers and get her blonde hair back. She smiled and said she would like that. Neither of them could believe the difference this made. It seemed to perk her up and remember some of who she used to be. She asked Sam if she used to be an attorney. He assured her that she was. She smiled.

Sam eventually told Allison about the phone call he received from a woman telling him where she was. She seemed to know immediately who that was. She said, "That was Kim, my friend Kim. I always knew she would help me if she could."

As the days, weeks and months went by, Sam watched baby steps as his wife returned to him. By this time, they were having meaningful conversations. Her memory was returning. She seemed to have more resilience to manage the flashbacks which continued to be so painful for her. There was evidence of her progress everyday. She was medicated everyday.

It had been a year since Allison had returned. Actually, she had returned in pieces. There were no words to describe the painful process of the year's events. Sam was very patient as she determined the things she was ready to talk about, and those she wasn't.

One night, in total surprise, Allison signalled that she wanted to have sex with Sam. He was shocked and unsure if she was really ready for this. To his amazement, it was a fabulous experience for both of them. It was like old times. He could hardly believe it. This was more progress than he could have imagined. It was like she had never left. He had never felt closer to her.

After that, things seemed to be better. She was better. They were better. Little Max started bringing his leash to her and she would take him for long walks. Sam could hardly believe it. It made him so happy. God had been so faithful to him. Mere Christianity was making more sense to him than he would ever have believed.

Sam asked Allison if she would like to take a trip with him to Hawaii. She smiled and said that sounded like a lovely idea. Sam booked the same suite they had enjoyed on their honeymoon. When they went into the room, Allison's eyes lit up and she remembered the special time they had there. She remembered their phenomenal week together.

The next day they went parasailing and had a fun day, just laughing and playing and drinking champagne. In fact, they were aware of just how much they had to celebrate. It was an incredible week. It was an incredible gift for both of them.

When they arrived home, things were more normal than Sam had remembered in a very long time. He was encouraged. Actually, it was time for Allison to testify at Ned's trial. She said she felt she was up to it.

On the stand she testified how Ned had come to their home that day. He told her Sam had been in a bad accident and that he was there to take her to him. As soon as she came out to get in his car, she had been taken.

She was whisked off to the airport, thrown on a private plane along with three other women and taken to a ship to meet a sheik. She had been servicing him for the past six years. The thought of him now made her nauseated. At the same time, she realized that it was the only thing that kept her alive. She looked at Ned in the courtroom that day, shook her head and said, "Shame, shame on you."

Sam was proud of her for testifying. She stayed in control, stated the facts and held herself together. This was much more than she could have done a year ago. She had come a very long way.

Eventually, Ned's trial led back to threats from the senator whom Sam had prosecuted earlier. Ten years was added to his sentence which pleased Sam immensely. Even those years could never be enough to pay for what his actions had done to Allison. He was an evil man. He could only imagine the damage he had done to numerous women over the years. It had to stop!

That night, Sam and Allison were having dinner. Sam had grilled steaks and they opened a special bottle of wine. Their conversation turned to their future. Sam asked Allison what she had left on her bucket list. Allison acknowledged to Sam that he had asked a very good question. She wished she had a very good answer. She said she would need to think about it. Sam smiled at her.

Sam and Allison were growing closer by the day. It was like they were falling in love all over again. Both of them were profoundly grateful for the renewing of their loving relationship. They really believed God had answered their prayers.

Little Max brought his leash into the kitchen and dropped it at Allison's feet. He wanted to go for a walk. Even though they usually walked him in the morning, they decided to take him for a short walk. It was a beautiful evening. They held hands as they walked. It felt like God was in His heaven and all was right with the world, a rare feeling for them both.

*****

This was trauma revisited for both Sam and Allison. They had just survived six of the worst years of their lives. They were both certain nothing could ever be as difficult as surviving their childhood traumas. They were wrong. Neither of them would ever be the same again.

The beauty of all of this pain was the bond of love between Sam and Allison. It has brought them through unbelievable suffering on their crooked path.

For all of their strengths and assets, these horrific acts still crushed them. What a difficult lesson to be learning at this stage of their lives. In spite of everything, they were determined to let each day unfold and do the best they could. They had both lived this nightmare before and now they were having to do it again.

They were grateful for the strength to even try. They were fighting for their lives.

CHAPTER 13

The Sheik?

The next morning, Allison made coffee and they were sitting out on the deck. She looked at Sam and said, "I've figured out the answer to your question." Sam looked puzzled. "My bucket list...you asked me what I had left on my bucket list." She went on to explain.

"Sam, I'd like for us to take a cruise together. We've never done that before. I think I'd like to take a cruise through the inside passage of Alaska. What do you think?" Sam smiled and said, "Love, if it's on your bucket list, I can't wait to get there."

Sam called their travel agent that afternoon and inquired about cruises to Alaska. He got the schedule and was happy to check some dates with Allison. They agreed and scheduled a seven day cruise for the fourth of July. They were both looking forward to it. Actually, Sam was a little surprised that Allison would have any interest in getting back on a ship after her experience in Qatar. However, he didn't mention that.

Before they knew it, it was time to enjoy their cruise. They boarded and were surprised at their beautiful stateroom.. It had a private balcony. Sam had booked a very special room. He was constantly demonstrating his love for her. She loved that about him. They stood on the balcony together as the ship left the harbor. It was going to be a great week. They were sure of it.

They were seated at dinner with six other couples. They were all from different parts of the country. They seemed like nice people. Dinner was excellent as was the company. Sam and Allison were the last to leave the table. It was a short distance to the elevator. They were ready to retreat to their lovely room.

As they stood waiting for the elevator, Allison thanked Sam for bringing her there. It was lovely and she was feeling very relaxed and happy to be there.

At that moment, the elevator door opened. Sam watched as all of the blood drained from Allison's face. She turned deathly white. Then, she took a second look and realized it wasn't him but he looked very much like him. She felt shaken, but incredibly relieved. She could hardly catch her breath.

When they were back in their room Allison said to Sam, "I thought it was him! I thought he was on this ship. Oh my God." She started shaking. Sam asked, "Who is on this ship?" Allison had started to cry and could barely answer him. When she caught her breath she whispered, "the sheik."

It was midnight and Allison was sound asleep. Sam was sitting out on the deck, racking his brain trying to formulate the best plan of action. It made him realize how seriously traumatized Allison still was and how much help she still needed.

The next morning, they had breakfast in their room out on the patio. It was a beautiful day. Sam was working extra hard to appear calm. Allison said she just wanted to get off the ship at the next port and fly home. Sam responded calmly by asking her if she really thought that was the best they could do. Allison looked at him with tears in her eyes and said she couldn't think of anything "best" right now. She was feeling unsafe and terrified. She just wanted to go home. Even though she realized it was not the sheik, it had set off an uncontrollable anxiety in her that was unmanageable. She felt out of control. She was fearful her panic attacks would return. She knew her fears were not rational but she could not wish them away.

Sam rang the bell of reality. He assured Allison that the sheik was not on this ship. He suggested they go together to see the ship's physician and get her some medication to help her calm down. This seemed to comfort her.

They had dinner in their room that night. It was lobster and it was excellent. They ate on the patio. Sam hated the tension they both felt.

Sam understood completely why Allison, although totally irrational, was too afraid to leave the room. He wasn't upset with her. He hated knowing there was a guy on the ship who looked like her tormentor and he couldn't do anything about it.

Allison took two of the pills the doctor had given her and fell asleep. Sam was wide awake and about to spend another sleepless night. He was hating this guy more by the minute., whoever he was.

Finally, it was the last night before the ship docked in the morning. They had survived the week, just barely. Allison took her last two pills and had fallen asleep. Sam was more than ecstatic that they were finally going to get off that ship. He never wanted to set foot on another one. So much for finishing up the bucket list!

The ship pulled into port. Sam had taken their luggage down the night before as requested by the ship's captain. Sam and Allison would be among the last ones to leave the ship. Allison was wearing dark clothes with sunglasses and a hat. She was lagging behind Sam as they shuffled their way to the exit. They got off the ship, retrieved their luggage and grabbed the first available taxi. They were headed home.

This had been one of the longest weeks of their lives. Sam didn't think he ever wanted to talk about it again. He wanted to just let it go and move on. This had been one of the worst experiences of his life. He was extremely angry.

They were very quiet on the flight home. They arrived in Seattle, gathered their luggage, found their car and headed home. They pulled into their garage and just sat there.

Finally, Sam said he thought it best if they didn't talk now, but rather wait until tomorrow. They were both very tired and neither wanted to say or do anything they would live to regret. They agreed, went to bed and fell asleep.

The next morning when Sam woke, Allison had prepared a lovely breakfast for them on the patio. She was dressed nicely and looked beautiful. Sam asked her if he had forgotten a special occasion. She said she felt so bad that she had ruined their cruise and this was her apology.

Sam immediately gave her a hug and said there was no apology needed. None of it was her fault. It was important to him that she knew how he felt. This is why she loved him so much. He was so deeply loving and understanding which was probably why she was feeling so guilty.

Allison had never spoken about what she experienced when she was kept by the sheik. She never would. She hoped Sam could understand by her reaction to seeing him again just how traumatized she was by that experience. Sam said he did understand and that he never wanted her to feel any pressure from him to talk about it.

Truth be known, with all of the stress they had managed, they were lucky they weren't divorced by now. They were both genuinely happy that had not happened to them.

Sam asked Allison if she would have any objections to him asking their private investigator friend to find out what he could about the sheik. Allison frowned and asked him why he would want to do that. Sam explained that maybe they were in a position to help women like she and Kim who had endured horrific suffering and trauma. Maybe there was a way to bring him to justice.

Allison said she appreciated Sam telling her about his idea but that if he decided to pursue it, she did not want to know anything about it. He agreed to those rules.

The next day, he called Greg, the incredible private investigator who found Allison. He inquired if he had time to take on a case. Greg said he could make time. It helped that he was already very familiar with this story, he would do what he could. Sam agreed. He told him about running into someone who looked a lot like him on the cruise ship in Alaska. He really wanted to find out all he could about this evil man.

Sam and Allison were getting back to their normal routine. Little Max continued taking his leash to them and enjoying their long walks. Allison was definitely feeling more and more relaxed. Their home felt calm and loving once again.

Sam had consented to taking on two new law cases. Both involved defending children. He had gotten quite comfortable with legal cases and family case law. Allison was always willing to help in any way she could. It was nice they could work together on projects that really mattered to them. It was part of the glue that kept them close to each other. Having children might have been part of that glue, also, but Allison's early sexual trauma made that impossible. The subject had only come up once between them. That was enough.

The next months were filled with work for Sam as he worked on his legal commitments. Allison had become more content to be at home with little Max. She had started a beautiful garden and was proud of all of the food they enjoyed as a result. She was becoming a gourmet cook and Sam was pleased to see her invested in projects she seemed to really enjoy.

Greg, unbeknown to Sam, was on the other side of the world in Qatar pursuing the sheik. He had learned a lot about him and had just located his current residence of which he had many. He owned several sizable yachts. They were all luxury liners, well stocked with females. He had taken many pictures of them. He would see they would be run through a database tracking missing females.

On the last day he planned to be there, he caught a break. The sheik left the yacht by himself. He had climbed onto a motor bike and was headed down the coast, along the ocean, toward the city. Greg followed him in his car. It was a very windy road, lots of steep curves along the ocean with no guard rails. There was very little traffic that day. Greg found himself going faster and faster, closing the distance between himself and the sheik.

Before he knew it, he had actually hit the motor bike and sent it flying off a cliff into the ocean far below. He stopped his car, turned off the engine and contemplated what he had just done. It was a surreal moment. He got out of the car, looked over the cliff and saw nothing. There was no one in sight. He got back into the car and drove to the airport. He was finished with this assignment.

His final report to Sam indicated that although he had located one of his ships and taken pictures of the females, there was nothing more to report. He had done what he could. Also, there was no charge. Sam would receive this report in the mail. He did not want to deliver it in person. He did not want to answer any questions about it.

Sam opened Greg's final report. He was surprised to see there was no charge. He was disappointed that Greg wasn't able to accomplish more, but was happy to get the pictures which might help identify some of the women. He had full confidence in Greg and had no reason to doubt his report.

Greg struggled with the way in which he handled this case. Part of him was deeply troubled by what he did. Another part of him was very pleased with ridding the world of such an evil man. Either way, God knew his heart and he was fully accountable. It was a secret he would take with him to his grave.

The following week, Sam was getting caught up on world news. Included in it was the alleged death of a very rich sheik from Qatar. This caught Sam's attention. It was simply reported that the man had disappeared and that his body was recovered from the ocean. It immediately crossed Sam's mind to ask Greg if he was aware of any of this. He decided Greg had enough on his mind and didn't need to have to answer any questions about it.

Sam printed out the story and the sheik's picture. When he got home later that day, he decided to ask

Allison if she recognized his picture. After dinner, he showed it to her. She screamed, "YES. That's him!!"

She burst into joyful tears! In that moment, she felt as though God had gifted her with an amazing gift. She felt beyond relieved. She felt vindicated. She felt happy for Kim and all the other victims he had traumatized and abused. It lifted her spirits more than anything she could remember. She felt as though she had just been released from death row.

Allison would never know the truth of the sheik's demise. She and Sam would just get to experience the freedom to live their lives without any fear of him. Allison was ready to book another cruise!

When Sam came home from work that night, Allison suggested to him that they book another cruise. He looked at her and said, "You must be joking." She smiled, fell into his arms and said she was very serious about it. She would go to the travel office tomorrow with her wide angle lens and see where it took her. Sam could see she was serious about it. He let her know it would have to be after his court cases were completed. It would be at least two months away. She smiled and said she totally understood. No problem.

*****

Allison's post traumatic stress was evidenced very strongly when she thought she was in the presence of the sheik. It indicated how much healing she still had in front of her.

Although she and Sam would never know the truth about the sheik's demise, she would always sleep better knowing he no longer existed. Maybe, finally, she can really let her guard down and be as fully available to Sam as she knew he deserved.

Although none of it was Allison's fault, she still felt guilt at all of the trauma and heartache she had brought to Sam's life. He deserved better. She deserved better! Now she was determined to find some kind of way to try to make some of it up to him.

Allison was very resourceful as was her love for Sam. She was looking for a special way to celebrate their twenty-fifth anniversary. She would find just the right magic.

CHAPTER 14

The Cruise

Allison came home from the travel office all excited. She believed she had found the perfect cruise. They would sail to London, the place where they first met and fell in love. Sam could see how excited she was. He agreed to go. He asked if they needed to screen all of the other passengers before boarding the ship. She laughed out loud.

The months went by quickly. Sam was in the final days of finishing up his trials. They seemed to be going well. They were scheduled to depart for their cruise in a few weeks. Sam had been working very hard and was ready for a vacation. This time, he hoped it would really be a vacation.

Allison had made all of the arrangements this time for the cruise. She had selected their room, late dining and had made several appointments for massages and salon treatments. This was going to be their trip of a lifetime. She wanted it to be a wonderful surprise for Sam. She wanted to look and be her absolute best for him. It was certainly what he deserved.

They had a neighbor with a little dog about Max's size. They loved to play together. She asked if they might keep Max while they went on their cruise. They said they would be happy to take care of him. She knew they were leaving Max in good hands.

Twas the night before they were to leave on their cruise. Allison had packed for both of them. She felt it was her turn to nurture Sam. It had always been the other way around. It was definitely his turn! She would do her very best.

They flew to New York and boarded the ship. As they made their way to their state room, they were aware of the beauty of the ship. It reminded them of pictures of the Titanic. They hoped it was built better! They didn't anticipate running into any icebergs as they made their way across the Atlantic. This was going to be a fantastic voyage.

As Sam unlocked the door to their stateroom, they were both taken back with surprise. They had a king bed, a beautiful balcony, fresh flowers and a bowl of fruit and a box of exquisite chocolates. It felt luxurious.

Allison took Sam by the hand and led him to the bed, removed her clothing and began removing his. The next thing they knew, four hours had passed and it was time for dinner. They showered together in a large glass shower. They took their time. They dressed and looked like they just stepped out of Vogue magazine. They were a gorgeous couple.

They held hands as they made their way to the dining room. They were booked at the second seating. They were joined by another couple. They were there first. They greeted them warmly. They were Jack and

Julie. They were all about the same age. They were from Sedona Arizona. They were both attorneys. Sam and Allison just looked at each other when they said it. Sam told them both of them were attorneys as well. Clearly, they all had a lot in common and a lot to talk about.

It was a very pleasant evening. The food was sumptuous, the conversation was lively and the libations were exceptional. Allison was already feeling five pounds heavier. They all felt so pleased that they had drawn such excellent company. They would look forward to seeing them tomorrow evening.

By this time it was 10PM. They were one of the last to leave the dining room. They decided to go into the main ballroom. They could hear beautiful music and people were dancing. Sam and Allison couldn't remember the last time they danced together. Before they knew it, it was midnight. It had been a magical evening.

As they undressed for bed, they both felt it had been an amazing day. They were both having massages first thing next morning, a couple's massage actually. Sam loved being surprised by all of Allison's efforts. He was loving every minute of it.

After their massages, they spent time in the spa. They steamed and spent time in the sauna. Finally, they took a swim in the beautiful pool. They were feeling absolutely relaxed. They moved to the deck by the ocean and enjoyed a salad and a glass of champagne. Allison couldn't stop looking at Sam. Her eyes filled with tears as she reached out and touched his hand. "I love you so much…..You are my love, my joy….my everything." Sam placed his other hand on hers, looked deeply into her eyes and simply smiled. They had been through so much together, and lived to tell about it. They were celebrating their 25th anniversary on Friday. Allison had already made special plans.

That evening, they were one of the best dressed couples in the dining room. They joined their new-found friends and thoroughly enjoyed the food and their company. Their conversations came easily and naturally. No one had to try to impress or one up in any kind of way. Everyone seemed at peace with themselves with nothing to prove.

Eventually, their conversation turned to their law careers. Allison shared that she and Sam were mostly invested in helping children. Jack said that he and Julie had spent the last decade prosecuting sex traffickers.

Allison nearly swallowed her fork. Summoning her courage, she inquired if they had followed the recent alleged death of a sheik in Qatar. They nodded affirmatively. They had even had a client whom they represented who had escaped his capture and prosecuted him. Sam asked how that trial ended. Jack explained it was mostly circumstantial and that he was acquitted.

The conversation changed as Allison raved about their couple's massage. She and Sam highly recommended it if there were still openings for appointments. Tomorrow, they were going to be part of a bridge tournament. They hadn't played in years but looked forward to just having fun and enjoying it. Actually, they ended up winning.

The rest of the week was filled with games and prizes. Everyone seemed to be having the time of their life. Allison and Sam took most of their lunches on the deck of their stateroom. It was such a pleasant place to be.

Tomorrow was their 25th wedding anniversary. Sam was in for some surprises. That morning, she asked him to come with her. She said she had a surprise. They left the room and made their way to the chapel. A very positive minister was waiting for them. Allison said she had made arrangements for them to renew their wedding vows. Sam locked eyes with her and gave her a big smile and a hug. They renewed their vows, with tears and great joy.

They had a special champagne lunch on their balcony and spent the rest of their day in that big beautiful king size bed. They continued drinking champagne and snacking on some belgian chocolates. Before they knew it, it was dinner time. Allison wore a beautiful green dress which matched her eyes. She wore a diamond choker Sam had given her on their 10th anniversary, with matching earrings. She looked absolutely stunning.

Sam couldn't have felt more proud than to have Allison on his arm. He felt he was the envy of every guy in the dining room. Why had God blessed him so beautifully? He felt overwhelmed with gratitude. He was finally starting to put the pieces of his life together in a way that made sense to him.

What a crooked path his life had been. There were just no words. He felt he was beginning to understand how C.S. Lewis had gone from being an atheist to becoming a Christian. What tangled lives we weave....

At dinner that night, Allison looked more radiantly beautiful than she had ever looked before. She was a blessing beyond description. He felt he was the luckiest man alive.

At dinner that night, they were served complimentary champagne, lobster and filet mignon. Their 25th anniversary was announced over the loudspeaker and the entire dining room clapped. It felt like a magical moment. It was everything and more that Allison had planned and hoped it would be. It was all God's gift to them. For all of the heartache, trauma and unbearable grief, they were experiencing more joy than either of them had ever known. Who understands the mind and ways of God?

That night, before they went to sleep, Sam and Allison had prayer together. Somehow it felt different than anytime before. Their words were brief, their hearts were overflowing, their love was stellar. It was the best of times.

One more day on the ship and they would be in London. Allison had made plans for them to stay two nights at the hotel where they first met. They would make a stop in Rome and in Athens before heading home. This really was the trip of a lifetime. She felt so blessed she had planned it and had the strength to enjoy it

The days passed quickly. They had time for a little bit of shopping in London. Allison purchased a beautiful little teapot and some exceptional teas. She also bought some scone mix. She bought some cookies and chocolate for the sweet neighbors tending to Max.

It was the last night before their flight back to Seattle. It had been the best time of their lives. It was a magnificent trip they would never forget. They had never felt closer. As they made love that last evening, it was expressed with more love than either of them had ever felt before. It really could never be any better than this.

As they boarded their flight for Seattle, there was a complete sense of satisfaction and grateful hearts for all they had experienced. This had been the best time of their whole lives. They both knew it.

It was a smooth flight back to Seattle. They were preparing to land. Allison noticed that Sam was not responding to the directive to fasten his seat belt. As she looked over at him, she could see his face was as white as a sheet. She shook him and he did not respond. He wasn't breathing.

She screamed, "Help us....somebody help us." The flight crew came running. There was an emergency page for any physician on board to please respond. Fortunately, there was a cardiologist seated behind them. He responded immediately. He placed Sam on the floor of the airplane and began giving him CPR. He requested oxygen for Sam and it was provided. He could only find a very faint pulse. Sam was in full cardiac arrest. It didn't look good.

The plane landed. The paramedics raced on board and removed him by stretcher. Allison quickly followed and they were both put on an ambulance which was racing toward a hospital. He was hooked up to monitors and looked very pale and unconscious. Allison prayed with all of her heart that God would spare his life and allow them to have more days and years together.

Sam was declared deceased in the hospital emergency room. They tried for 30 minutes to shock his heart and revive him. It wasn't to be. He was gone.

There were no words to describe what Allison was feeling. She was numb. She felt paralyzed. She was dumbfounded. She didn't understand. This was the worst day of her life!

*****

Allison and Sam had just spent the finest week of their marriage together. Their love had never been more precious or celebrated. How could it possibly be over?

Allison felt betrayed. Her whole life had been filled with trauma. Sam was the greatest gift she had ever known. They had survived hell and had moved heaven and earth to be together. Did God really give him this expiration date? There must be some mistake.

Grief is a formidable opponent. It never feels fair. Sometimes it doesn't even feel survivable. Sometimes it makes us feel like nothing matters anymore. These feelings make for very difficult days. Death becomes seducing and difficult to resist.

Allison was in the fight of her life. Not only was she in a relationship crisis, she was in a faith crisis. What kind of God allows people like Sam and Allison to suffer so greatly? Then, when they finally find hope and love, it ends. She felt numb.

Death was looking good to Allison. Her one concern was little Max. Who would look after him and love him as much as she did? She knew the answer. She never really believed she would deliberately end her life but she already felt dead inside.

Allison lost weight, had trouble sleeping and wasn't seeing anyone. She barely got the bills paid. She was sinking fast and she knew it

CHAPTER 15

Making Sense of the Crooked Path

In the weeks and months that followed, Allison was challenged with the greatest grief of her life. She wanted to die.

Her only connection was with little Max. He kept her going and got her out of the house each day for their walk. Allison let her garden die, did not answer her phone or bother to get the mail. She was beyond devastated. She couldn't even remember life before Sam.

She went to the cemetery everyday and had long talks with Sam. She would stay there for hours at a time. She was out of control.

It took many months before she was able to function. Even coming home from Qatar was easier than this. How could God possibly expect her to survive life without Sam?

Allison would always be grateful for the incredible last days they had together. They were magical and she would always treasure them. Now she had to find a way to keep going, but it really felt like an impossible dream. She simply didn't know how to do life without Sam. Allison realized their last trip together had been God's great gift to them. She was really clear about that and would always be grateful. She also knew in her heart that only God holds the keys to life and death. How grateful she needed to be that she was able to celebrate 25 years of marriage with this incredible human being.

Allison knew that with Sam's death, there were some very important legal decisions she needed to make. Sam's estate was in her hands now. She felt the need to seek legal counsel and financial assistance in order to make wise decisions. Very slowly, she was trying to put one foot in front of the other. She tried to think of consultants she could trust, consultants Sam and Arthur would trust. Finally she made some calls and set up some appointments.

Allison put all of their assets into Arthur's foundation. At her death, everything was to go to the Arthur Adams Foundation. She was trying hard to make her decisions the way she thought Sam would have wanted. This decision would ensure the longevity and support for helping children, something with which she and Sam and Arthur would all agree. She and Sam had never talked about their deaths.

The pieces were starting to fall into place. She was simply going through the motions. She felt the same way she did when she returned from Qatar, barely conscious. This time, she didn't have Sam's arms to fall into. There were just no words for the emptiness she was feeling. This was a depth of grief she never knew existed. She didn't know how she was going to make it through the next five minutes. She knew she needed help.

Allison made an appointment with the pastor from Sam and Arthur's church. She tried to communicate what she was experiencing but the words just wouldn't come. She couldn't even find the words. There were no words. She left feeling very empty.

About all that kept her going these days was little Max. He was a very senior dog by now and no longer brought her his leash. A few days a week, they would take a short walk and could sometimes make it around the block. She couldn't even imagine what she was going to feel when he was gone. It brought tears to her eyes to even think about it. She knew it was coming. She would have to deal with it. She would feel jealous that he would be with Sam again, something she wanted with all her heart.

Allison hadn't touched the clothes in his closet. She hadn't parted with anything that had been his. Sometimes she would go into their closet and just hold a piece of clothing that still had his scent on it. Sometimes she would sleep with it. She was experiencing pathological grief.

Things finally got so bad Allison made an appointment with her physician. He immediately prescribed antidepressant medication and some sedatives to help her sleep. He actually considered admitting her to a mental hospital for 30 days for grief therapy. He was very concerned about her stability. She had lost 30 pounds and looked very gaunt.

She explained to him that she had a beloved dog at home and was very committed to caring for him. This was actually true. Somehow, Allison was thinking she would have Max buried next to Sam. Sam would like that.

Allison's neighbors reached out to her but she didn't reach back. She told them she was OK and thanked them for their concern. She was grateful for them and knew she could turn to them if she really needed help.

In the past 25 years, Sam had become Allison's entire life. She had no parents, no siblings, deceased grandparents, no aunts and uncles or cousins. She had no family. Sam was her world. He was her life. He was her everything.

One night, after endless hours of crying, Allison reached for Sam's Bible. She hadn't really been talking to God lately. She really hadn't felt like it. Actually, she stumbled onto some lines Sam had underlined. They were from Proverbs: "Trust in the Lord with all your heart and lean not unto your own understanding. In all your ways, acknowledge Him and He will direct your path."

Allison began to digest this verse. She was low on trust, didn't trust her heart with anyone but Sam, had next to no understanding of her life's events and she felt clueless as to how to acknowledge Him and get direction. Somehow, this just didn't get it for her. It caused her to realize just how depressed she really was.

Allison had only been taking the antidepressants for a week and knew it would take longer than that before they would do her any good. She hoped she could hang on for that long. She realized she was losing her will to live. She really didn't care about anything anymore. Without

Sam, life just didn't make sense. She knew everyone came with an expiration date, but she just couldn't accept that this was Sam's.

For the first time, Allison approached Sam's desk. She had never done that before. She shuffled through several legal documents which she recognized. Finally, in the bottom right-hand drawer, she pulled out a book with the title, "Journal" on the front. She opened it. She was not aware of Sam keeping a journal.

She had no idea where Sam would have found time to actually record in a journal. She was intrigued as she read his entries. The last one had been made the day before they left on their cruise. Sam had written:

1. I need to take responsibility for my part of the events in my life. I need to realize the dysfunction of my choices, seek to remedy them and stay focused on whatever it requires of me to make them right.

2. I need to learn how to reframe things. I need to understand that everyone has their own version of reality that seems right to them. Sometimes I need a mirror held up to me to understand my own need to change. I need to admit when I'm wrong.

3. I need to work to separate people from their behavior. Doing a bad thing is not the same as being a bad person. I understand this from my relationship with Ned. He did a bad thing. He wasn't a bad person. Understanding this reality might help me work on forgiveness.I need to stop judging and work on understanding.

4. I need to pay attention to unfinished business. Do things exist that I still have the power to change, such as asking forgiveness or offering support to someone who needs it? I need to make the changes that are still in my power to choose. I will not always have time.

5. What am I pretending not to know? Blurring the truth can sometimes help me feel better momentarily but I will likely pay for it in the long run.

6. What detours am I still taking in order to avoid things I don't want to believe? What price am I paying for being on this detour? How far back is it to the main road where I can find my balance?

7. Am I really committed to doing what I need to create a new reality? I need to seek peace and pursue it.

8. Do I believe in myself? If not, what do I need to change?

9. Giving up is never really a good option. How do I reach out and ask for help when I feel like quitting.

10. Who am I still blaming? When will I stop keeping score and stop justifying my anger?

11. What are my goals? What do I still have on my bucket list?

12. I am not alone. There is always hope. I need to remember this. My faith in God is what keeps me going.

13. Have I given away my powers to people who don't deserve them, who shouldn't have them? How do I take them back? What would that look like?

14. Death is not my enemy. It is a transition to be made with as few regrets as possible. I can do this!

15. At the end of every day, no matter what, I am my choices and must take responsibility for them.

16. Life is now. Now is all I have. It is all I will ever have.

17. At the end of my life, I will have gotten to wherever I am, one choice at a time. I must own it. I must own my crooked path. I must own the fact that I cannot unring any of the bells in my life. It is what it is. I must always focus forward.

Allison finished reading, put the journal down and covered her face with her hands. She sobbed for several minutes. She wanted to think about, understand and digest the mind and heart of Sam.

Even more importantly, she needed to find a way to apply his truths in her own life. This would take a very big effort on her part. She would read and contemplate them every day. These entries represented Sam's deepest thoughts and goals of his life. They deserved her committed attention.

As the week progressed, Allison worked hard to grasp the meaning of Sam's journal entries. Very slowly, she had begun making subtle changes in her own life.

She knew how invested Sam was in Arthur's Foundation. Maybe that would be a good place for her to start. She hadn't been there in many months. Perhaps she would go there the following morning.

It was very hard for her to drive through the iron gates, up the driveway and find her way into the study. She just sat there quietly for several minutes, in Sam's chair. She could feel the presence of Sam and Arthur. It was palpable. They had so many productive meetings in that very room. They had accomplished so many positive things. They had strategized and won important cases. It was a place of hope, a place for problem solving, a place for renewal. It felt good to her to be there. It was the same place where she and Sam had their first meeting.

It was also a place where little broken children came to find hope and begin a new life. She saw them playing in the yard as she looked out the window of the study. It gave her pause.

Was her pain any greater than theirs? Was she having an unending pity potty that she needed to snap out of? Would Sam want her to simply give it all up because he couldn't be there anymore? She hated but knew the answers.

Allison thought back about Sam's life after she had been kidnapped. He spent 6 years without her. Had he thrown in the towel and given up? Just what kind of a message would she be giving to the young children who came to the foundation for help if she gave up? Sam and

Arthur would not want that. Even more, God would not want that. The last thing she would ever want to do was hurt or disappoint Sam in any way.

For the first time since he died, Allison was able to get a glimpse of her grieving self and get perspective on where her choices were taking her. She was on a deadly path. These were not the choices Sam would have made nor were they choices he would have wanted her to be making. Allison was beginning to feel this was a serious wake-up call for her. It felt as though someone was holding up a giant mirror in front of her and she didn't like what she saw.

Both Allison and Sam had enormous challenges in their lives. Who gets kidnapped twice? How is life fair? How are people supposed to survive the heinous things that happen to them? Somewhere in Allison's heart, she knew the answer. She knew that God had entrusted both of them with incredible gifts, in spite of all their pain. God had brought the broken pieces of their lives and woven them together and led them on their crooked path.

She wondered why she could not see that her faith promised her that she would see Sam again? Life is not fair. God never said it would be: "In this world you will have tribulation. I have overcome the world." We either believe it or we don't.

Allison's brain was flooded with thoughts: Her faith was challenged. Bad things happen to good people. Life is not fair. Broken hearts are a way of life. Losing people we love hurts us and may destroy us if we let it. People deceive us, betray us. Is there anyone we can trust? These facts challenge all of us everyday. There are no simple or easy answers. We either choose to keep fighting or we choose to give up. It's up to us.

At that moment, the door to the study flung open. Standing in the door was one of the children. He was crying. He looked at Allison and asked, "Where's my Mommy?" Almost without thinking, Allison simply opened her arms to him. He fell into them. He sobbed for several minutes as Allison just held him. This was something that had been done for her many times. She understood exactly what this little guy was feeling.

When the crying let up, she picked him up and held him on her lap. She began asking him questions. He looked at her and put his thumb in his mouth. He threw his other arm around her neck, buried his little head in her chest and continued sobbing. This was surreal for Allison. It was like a total role reversal. She totally identified with what this little guy was feeling. Eventually, he stopped crying. She did her best to help calm him. She took him by the hand and led him down the hall to the kitchen where they could find ice cream.

This little guy's name was Tommy. He was new here. His "angel" had lost track of him but saw them and followed close behind not saying anything. Allison helped him get an ice cream cone. It was his favorite flavor. Eventually the three of them spent a little time together until he was feeling better. At that time, his caretaker took him by the hand and led him out to the courtyard. Allison just stood and watched. She realized she also wanted a caretaker, someone who would take her by the hand and lead her out of the shadows and into the light. Her eyes filled with tears as she found her way back into the study.

Allison's head was full of thoughts. Everyone has times in their life when they feel like giving up. Get in line. God brought Sam and Allison through extremely difficult circumstances, including the loss of parents through death and suicide, kidnap and torture, sexual and drug abuse, betrayals by Christian friends, loss of loved ones through death. These were, sadly, all part of their crooked path together.

C.S. Lewis and Sam both found their path to God by weaving their way through the tangled losses in their lives. There weren't any easy answers. There still aren't. There aren't any angels bouncing off the wall or messages from God in the sky. That isn't who God is or how he works. We walk by faith. We all have a crooked path.

God used Sam's death as an important marker in Allison's life. He gave him to her and He took him away! That power belongs to Him, no one else. We never know what His timing will be. We should never take time, or people, for granted. It is our job to trust Him, no matter what.

Allison felt as though she had just had a meeting with God Himself. He had spoken to her, through Sam, Arthur and little Tommy. It was palpable. She was getting a glimpse of what her choices needed to be, what she needed to do and the changes she needed to make.

Allison realized that she had gotten through all of the painful experiences in her life because of her faith in God. Why should now be any different? She needed to understand that Sam was still with her. He would always be with her.

Some part of Allison knew that God would give her the strength to face her fears and find the will to keep going in spite of her loss. Sam would always be her everything. God understood that. Allison was so busy mourning Sam's death that she was ignoring what didn't die. This thought made her smile. There were so many beautiful things about Sam that Allison treasured in her heart.

In that moment, Allison realized how poorly focused she had been and how unhealthy her choices had been. As she looked out the window and saw the children, she wanted to start spending time there. She wanted to get to know little Tommy. She wanted to get personally involved with Arthur's Foundation and help them in any way she could. She wanted to start putting her energies where they could do some good. It occurred to her that these realizations were a profound answer to her prayers. Enough of grief and heartache! Sam wanted so much better for her!

The one project that she and Sam had completed was their work with the children. She allowed herself to feel those old and beautiful feelings. Allison chose to deal with her grief, even though it felt beyond her control. She allowed herself to move out of the shadows and into the light. Ultimately, Allison was challenged to move out of her own pain and direct her energies toward helping others. This was the positive choice that would help her heal. It felt right. She could feel Sam smiling at her.

Allison arrived back home, scooped little Max up in her arms and held him tight. It was a new day. It would be a new path. It would be a new life. After all, God was the Creator who brought her and Sam together and walked with them through their crooked path. He wasn't going anywhere. He had walked Sam to his journey's end and was waiting to walk Allison to hers.

The crooked path is the God-given destiny we all walk. We are never alone on the crooked path. He always walks with us. There always exists an extra set of footprints. We don't always see or feel them. We can walk with hope, joy and expectation, knowing that God is shaping our crooked path according to His design.

As the clock is ticking, may we focus forward and hold our feet strong to the design of our crooked path, knowing we are never alone on our journey.

AUTHOR'S CONCLUSIONS

Life will always be a crooked path for all of us.

No matter who we are or what path we are on, it will always have surprises. Much of it is out of our control. What we do have control of is our responses to those events. We have created all of the responses to our crooked path.

Sam and Allison's lives included one trauma after another. How they dealt with each of those events defined their crooked path, their relationship and their destiny.

None of us can know in advance who will cross our path or when, or even why, for that matter. We don't know what the impact will be on our life. Our choices are based on our experiences and therefore our environment and the people in it are critical in determining our destiny. We cannot predict it with any certainty if we're really honest.

Life is about making choices from the alternatives we perceive. Our perceptions are critical. They are determined by many things, including our intelligence, timing, our core belief system and by who we have been programmed to be.

Change is one of the hardest, most feared and least understood pieces of our path. It's up to us to make the choice and determine how crooked our path will be. Special strength is given by focusing on and understanding there are always two sets of footprints on our path, no matter what! We are not alone.

Whatever path on which we find ourselves, we got there one choice at a time. It is a path of our making. For our part, we can make it as smooth or as crooked as we desire. We need to remember that whatever choices we are making, it is all being done in a timetable that will always represent the unknown.

We must tread with caution and confidence, putting one foot in front of the other, trusting the ground to be there. We must learn to embrace our crooked path and hold it dear.

Sam knew who he was. He learned how to cherish every day and weigh every choice wisely. Finally, he reached his last time to choose.

Sam's life ended, but his beautiful crooked legacy will last forever.

CPSIA information can be obtained
at www.ICGtesting.com
Printed in the USA
LVHW110144140821
695160LV00004B/428